My Samoan Chief

My Samoan Chief

FAY G. CALKINS

WITH DRAWINGS BY MIRCEA VASILIU

University of Hawaii Press
Honolulu

This edition published by arrangement with Doubleday & Company

Library of Congress Catalog Card Number 76–149794
ISBN 0–87022–932–X
Printed in the United States of America

05   04   03   13   12   11   10

University of Hawai'i Press books are printed on acid-free paper and
meet the guidelines for permanence and durability of the Council on
Library Resources.

TO MY MATAI

without whom this book would obviously
never have occurred to me.

CONTENTS

CHAPTER ONE

Library of Congress

I squinted through my glasses, clutched my zipper notebook, and hoped I would pass as an egghead. The dome
of the Library of Congress looked very awesome from underneath as I tiptoed around the great circular call desk and
back through the card catalogues. In a whisper I asked a
guard for the stacks and showed him my three-month permit to a desk on deck A. It was only a student desk, and I
can't say I really needed a seat among the political science
treatises, but I thought the atmosphere might lend a more
academic tone to my field notes. At least in the stacks
there would be fewer distractions.

With this in mind I boarded the small stack elevator
along with a bearded professor, and innocently rose to the
spot which led me not to an academic career, but to a banana plantation in the rain forests of Samoa.

An elderly librarian snapped on the light of my green
metal desk. It was remote all right. I peered down dim cor-
ridors of books in all directions. The only other sign of human habitation was a desk like mine a few feet away, but
empty, and a row of glass cubicles for the intellectual elite
along the walls. I settled down comfortably into my chair.

The little old librarian leaned over confidentially. "Let me give you a piece of advice," he said. "I see many students come in here to write dissertations. Some get to like it too much. Why, right over there," and he pointed to a glass cubicle, "is a man who came in to write an exhaustive dissertation on the Treaty of Berlin. That was forty years ago. He found all knowledge was related and is still working on it. My advice is, get yours done quickly."

Even as he spoke a dried-up figure with a dusty bald spot and a green eyeshade trotted up the stacks under a load of books. Without so much as a glance in our direction he dived into his glass cubicle and slammed the door. I was stunned. I not only finished my thesis in three months but have never been in a library stacks since.

In the next few days I discovered that I was surrounded not only by books but by some colorful neighbors. An energetic nun held court in a cubicle behind me. She was writing a critique of Fabian socialism but a daily procession of depressed-looking individuals managed to elude the library guards and knock at her door for tearful conferences.

In a cubicle to my right I caught glimpses of a wild thatch of hair. It belonged to a wiry professor who had been born in Eastern Europe and who specialized in Russia.

"I want your opinion on this," he called to me one day. Flattered, I hurried over. He had just translated an article from *Pravda*, something about "diabolical American imperialism."

"What does that mean to you?" he asked handing me the translation. The sentiment was not an unusual one for *Pravda* so I could only conclude that he was testing me rather than the material.

"Oh nothing at all," I muttered fearfully, wondering if my stacks permit would be canceled. He sighed at the abysmal ignorance of the American collegiate mind and let me go.

In front of the professor was an ardent Chinese scholar. He had discovered that the Library of Congress had several hundred years of birth records from county courthouses in China. Since their originals had been destroyed he was here compiling population statistics.

An even more poetic individual came regularly to the student lunchroom. He affected bare feet and a full beard and ate only a single avocado, speared with a small dagger which he carried at his belt.

For weeks the student's desk next to mine in the middle of deck A remained empty. I felt slightly lonesome in this vast sea of learning.

Then I became aware of increasing activity beside me. It wasn't as if a student came in, sat down, and began to study. At first it was just a chicken bone in the wastebasket, or a light left on at the desk. Sometimes in the mornings I found books and papers strewn about. Finally, one evening a young man appeared and started rummaging through the drawers. If something was going on at that desk it clearly wasn't a concerted intellectual effort. I finally asked the librarian if the desk had been assigned.

"It's someone with an unpronounceable name," he told me, "from some island somewhere. But I never see him around, do you?"

I said I had only noticed symptoms, but would keep my eyes open. Soon I discovered that my elusive neighbor was not one, but two or three individuals. It was hard to tell exactly because they all looked alike: tall, copper-colored, black-eyed, wavy-haired, and undeniably handsome.

One afternoon all three arrived at once. The effect was ;nore animation than the political science treatises had seen in some time. There was an argument, then great chuckling, and even, if I am not mistaken, a snatch of song—all in a language completely incomprehensible to me. There certainly was no reference to the books at hand.

I watched with interest from a distance of about six feet, but my neighbors seemed neither disturbed by my attention nor aware of my existence. The librarian scuttled down the corridor gesticulating wildly. They moved off gaily leaving a ukulele on the desk.

"Did they disturb you?" the librarian asked me anxiously, thinking, no doubt, of my three-month deadline.

"I love to be disturbed," I sighed, and wondered if they would come back again.

Next morning the neighboring desk was empty but I was surprised to find an unfamiliar book on the middle of my own. I was even more surprised to find it was not about local politics, Fabian socialism, American imperialism, or the population of China. It was an intriguing legend about a beautiful girl, attired only in her long blond hair, who could be seen of an evening flitting around a tropical jungle. If visiting sailors gave chase the legend didn't exactly specify what happened, but they were invariably found strangled. I was perplexed as to the significance of all this.

A few days later I was about to return the legend to a more suitable section of the library when one of my handsome neighbors appeared at his desk. In a flash of inspiration I took the book over to him.

"Did you lose this book?" I inquired slowly in case he didn't speak English.

"No, I didn't lose it," he replied casually, "I left it there for you to read."

I was impressed. "It's quite a story," I stammered.

"It's not a story at all," he retorted. "It is perfectly true. I know a soldier who saw that girl and he died."

I sat down suddenly on the stool beside his desk. "Where did all this happen?"

"In Samoa," he replied. "This marine and I were on guard up in the mountains and we both saw her running around, just like it says. This other fellow was after her in a flash, but not me—I'm not that type. Next morning we found him—strangled."

"Were you really in Samoa?" I asked breathlessly.

"That is my home," he replied with some dignity.

I probed my mind for something about Samoa but all I could recollect were some interesting customs of Samoan adolescents observed by Margaret Mead. Since this was not material for further conversation at this point in our acquaintance, I simply asked, "What is your name?"

"My name is Ala'i—just cough between the 'a' and the 'i'," he said with an engaging smile. "But I suggest you call me Vai and come out for a coke."

In deference to the Samoan economy it turned out that the coke was on me. But it was a worthwhile investment.

I found that Samoa was several tropical islands, fourteen degrees south of the equator, in the western Pacific. Vai had been born on the largest of these islands in an open-sided house thatched with sugar-cane leaves. He was the oldest of ten full-, plus four half-brothers and sisters. Just a nice, ordinary Samoan family. His childhood had been a glorious succession of feasts, church festivals, and visiting parties in war canoes, without the inconvenience of going to school. His only serious trial was having to wear clothes, since his father was a Methodist pastor. Certainly his past had bequeathed him a most sociable personality.

When he was twelve his father had been transferred to the smaller but more sophisticated island of Tutuila which was serving as an American naval base. Here Vai began school. If he missed the school boat, as often happened, he had to swim a mile across the bay with his slate and *lavalava* (skirt-cloth) in his teeth. Tutuila was mountainous and crowded. Taro, the starchy tuber which is the mainstay of the Samoan diet, was not as easy to come by as on the lusher island of Savaii. Money was more essential. Released from traditional Samoan life, Vai soon fell in with the cosmopolitan elements around the waterfront. His career might have ended right there if he had not happened to get a job as caddy for the navy Captain of the Yard. This captain and his wife took an interest in their happy-go-lucky caddy. For the first time in his life Vai found himself getting regular meals, which he ate in their kitchen, and regular sessions at the village school. He actually found he liked school. In six years he put himself through nine grades and formed a tenuous acquaintance with the English language. He wanted more, but Tutuila had no high school, and he had no money to go elsewhere. Vai had to content himself with teaching the grade from which he had just graduated.

When World War II broke out there were suddenly more Americans than Samoans on the rocky little island. Life changed, particularly the wage scale. With an elementary knowledge of building thatched huts, Vai got a job as carpenter, building navy installations. The experience was more satisfactory to Vai than to the Navy, however, which never felt as he did about Samoan feasting. In order to avoid an unpleasant encounter with the military police on this subject, Vai hastily joined a unit of Samoan marines which was then in the process of formation.

In addition to an intimate acquaintance with the topography of Samoa, the United States Marines left Vai one important gift—thirty-seven months of the GI Bill, a chance to go to school, the very thing he had been looking for.

A friendly harbor pilot slipped him aboard a freighter bound for Honolulu. There one of his old teachers steered him to Lahaina Luna, a farm school on the island of Maui, where he could go to high school and support himself by collecting eggs.

Lahaina Luna was a wise choice. Vai had good teachers and plenty of friends but little time for the bright lights and soft music that so often tempt the unwary and lighthearted. Up at five, eggs till seven, school until three, eggs again until five, supper at six, then homework. The chickens even laid eggs on Sunday! Samoa was never like this. But somehow Vai survived a year and a half and came out with a high school diploma, a lingering nostalgia for ukuleles and knife dancing, United States naturalization papers, and a yen to go to college.

Thanks to the chickens Vai had not yet used his GI Bill, but again it was a problem of transportation. A brief experience in a cannery convinced him that pineapples were even more demanding than chickens. A friend induced him to try a more exciting pursuit—boxing. Though completely innocent of this Western art, Vai was by nature endowed with long arms, a hard head, and a way with the grandstand. At his first bout, after a few hard knocks he held his own, took half the purse, and was on his way to the mainland next morning.

This time he found his way to a small college run by the Brethren in the middle of Kansas. Again it turned out to be a good choice. Classes were small so that he got personal attention. Standards of conduct were so well defined that he had a chance to learn Western ways without too much scope for experimentation. Kansas was not blessed with many Samoans, so Vai's convivial weakness for Samoan feasting was not put to the test. Under the circumstances he had to learn English. He met with little race prejudice and soon felt quite at home with his fellow students. He wasn't always so much at home with term papers—but even in such matters a Samoan smile carries weight. He came through with a B.A. in history within his thirty-seven GI months.

By now Vai had guessed that the New World was larger than a Brethren community in Kansas, and he prepared to see more of it. He spent one summer in Mexico and another at the University of California at Berkeley. Then he decided to visit his old friend, the Captain of the Yard, in Washington, D.C. The captain encouraged his desire for more education. But this time Vai wanted to study something that would take him back to Samoa in a useful capacity. He settled down for a year of graduate work in public administration at American University in Washington.

With no GI Bill and no chickens, he once more faced the problem of supporting himself. For one harrowing week he struggled with luggage at Union Station. Then he had a go at dishwashing and knife dancing. Finally one of his professors directed him to a position as job analyst in the Classification and Wage Administration Branch of the U. S. Air Force.

This job turned out to be the happiest of all his experiences in America. Not only did it support him, it gave his public administration studies a specific bent which suited his own inclinations. Personnel work in the Air Force was a highly technical pursuit, but apparently this did not rob the staff of a human interest in employees. Maybe they were interested in training somebody for Samoa, maybe they were just captivated by that Samoan smile. In any case they took some pains to help Vai. During working hours the staff gave him close supervision and increasingly heavy assignments. They sent him to special training courses, speeded up his reading, and presented him with a set of technical books. In addition that office seemed to have a good time outside of working hours, and they readily included Vai with his knife dances and war chants. He soon concluded that personnel work was the right thing for him.

Washington is not like Kansas. Samoans do pass through from time to time. Whenever they did, they shared Vai's lodging, clothing, friends, and other assets in true Samoan fashion. By the time Vai had finished his exams and was thinking about his master's thesis, two other Samoans had arrived in Washington to share his air force income and his room. It was for privacy that Vai applied for a desk at the Library of Congress, though he scarcely had time to use it. Quite naturally his desk was soon shared by all Samoans.

For the price of one coke, I felt I now understood my neighbors better, though I might not be able to explain them clearly to the librarian.

But I felt something else as well. Was it possible that I, too, should be captured by that Samoan smile?

CHAPTER TWO

Courtship—Samoan Style

Our new friendship undoubtedly benefited Vai's thesis more than it did mine; at least he turned up at his desk more often. My knowledge of Samoan custom grew faster than my chapters on political action.

The first thing I learned was that Samoans really do share anything they get as soon as they get it and often before they pay for it. As a result they are always broke and glad to share whatever anyone else happens to have at the moment. My father happened to have a car and it was soon in constant service transporting Samoans here and there.

One evening it took us to the station to meet Lafi, Vai's brother. Lafi was an imposing young man; so was his luggage—all sixteen pieces of it. He reminded me of visiting royalty and he soon informed me that that was exactly what he was. He was closely related, he said, to Malietoa, paramount chief of Samoa. I could picture Lafi in full tribal regalia directing affairs of state. It was only later that I discovered Samoa has four paramount chiefs and that almost every Samoan is related to one of them.

Lafi's pocketbook unfortunately was not commensurate

with his dignity. It was not even capable of lodging him for a night. The floor of Vai's room could not sleep another body; his income could not fill another mouth. But this worried Lafi not in the least.

"All that is necessary," he told me, "is to drive me to the nearest Methodist minister. He is bound to take me in because my father is a Methodist pastor in Samoa."

The idea was new to me, but to my astonishment, apparently quite practical. Before evening Lafi was happily settled in the family of a Methodist minister in Bethesda.

One day Vai asked my mother if he could have a little party at our home to welcome his sister Lusi in real Samoan fashion. Of course my mother agreed and polished up her twelve place settings.

"How many are coming?" she inquired two days before the welcome.

"Oh, somewhere between fifty and seventy, I should say," Vai replied casually. "It's hard to tell exactly because for such things Samoans just turn up by themselves, you don't invite them."

"What do Samoans eat at such affairs?" asked my mother, aghast.

"Couldn't you get a couple of bunches of green bananas at your chain store?" suggested Vai. "And, you know, we need three roast pigs. It would be just the thing to make Lusi feel at home."

My mother is accustomed to three chops in a cellophane bag. "But Vai," she said, "I wouldn't know where to get a whole pig or how to cook one. I couldn't get more than one leg into my oven."

"Oh don't worry about the cooking," Vai said courteously, "boys always do that in Samoa. We will make an *umu* in your back yard."

"What is an *umu?*" my father inquired looking up from the evening paper.

"It's the way we cook things in Samoa," Vai explained. "We pile a lot of rocks on an open fire. When they are hot we put the bananas and taros and pig on them and cover the whole thing with leaves and sacks. An hour later all the food is really delicious."

"Not in my back yard," announced my father firmly. He had spent all summer bringing our small strip of grass to perfection.

Since there was no practical way of modifying a list of uninvited guests, we decided to modify the food instead. Vai's second choice was chicken hecca, a Hawaiian dish. Unfortunately we didn't know how to make that either.

The administration of a Samoan feast was quite beyond my mother and me. We were worried sick just over the problem of seventy spoons. But not Vai. When our confusion finally dawned upon him he asked a Samoan friend to take over. She did so not only confidently but enthusiastically. On the day of the party she arrived with plenty of eating equipment, apparently borrowed from all her neighbors. She drafted early guests to cut up the vegetables and before long even my mother and I were enjoying the affair.

It *was* a small party by Samoan standards, but it had the desired effect on Lusi. The bewilderment and tension in her face relaxed into a warm smile as she saw the guests. She was a girl of commanding proportions, and apparently her unlikely purple sateen lavalava and sturdy bare feet had felt conspicuously unique on the long trip to America. But now they felt at home. She moved out into the crowd like a queen, head and shoulders above anyone else, nodding graciously here, chatting easily there, the picture of self-confidence. My mother and I felt like nervous little birds hopping along beside her.

Lusi stayed with us for several months before her school began, as charming a guest as one could imagine. Our only concern was to mold her to more American proportions. My mother's theory was that the difference was dietary, and Lusi tolerantly submitted to a regime that would have embarrassed the poorest Samoan hostess. She emerged a few weeks later, more willowy but somewhat less confident. I was assigned a more difficult task—footwear. Her feet had not shrunk. As cold weather approached this issue became critical. Lusi and I toured Washington. At each store a dapper little man trotted up to us. Tucking a little stool beneath him, and chattering away, he expertly reached for Lusi's leg. As its foot came to rest before him a look of incredulity invariably crossed his face. His hands retracted slowly and his clucking trailed away uncertainly.

"Now that's the way a foot should look." I told him to ease the silence. But he didn't seem to hear. He sat looking at the foot as if he couldn't believe it.

"You could have a foot like that too, if you would climb trees barefooted," I pointed out hopefully. His eyes traveled slowly down to his own tiny, shiny, pointed appendages tucked neatly under the stool.

Since this was as far as we usually got, we finally had a pair of shoes especially made for Lusi before she left for school.

I soon discovered that Samoans have a natural bent towards politics and away from economics. Lafi's first announcement after settling the lodging question was that he was going to spend his time "on Capitol Hill." To the consternation of the Department of the Interior which looks after wandering Samoans, he really meant it.

Congressmen, it turned out, were quite willing to listen to this young man from an island to which they donate over one million dollars a year. It was never clear to me exactly what Vai's brother Lafi was lobbying for, but he did seem to be on personal terms with an astonishing number of congressmen. He even suggested to the President whom he should appoint as governor.

His political success did not ingratiate him with the Department of the Interior. When he proposed to bring over eight more relatives, the Office of Territories put its foot down, and even threatened to send him home. But Lafi not only stayed—he brought his relatives.

Vai's interests were more international. He was distressed at the long-standing division of the Samoan islands between the United States and New Zealand. The idea of a condominium appealed to him and he informed the United Nations accordingly.

Economics, however, especially of the personal variety, escaped them all. In alarm at the problem of supporting a tribe on one person's income, I suggested a budget.

"Why make problems?" Vai said. "Don't you believe in God?"

God certainly did His best for Samoans, but even His omnipotence was tested in the case of Lafi's car.

Lafi needed a car for his political activities, and he got one with a little down and plenty to go. Unfortunately he was not as sophisticated with car dealers as he was with congressmen. Next day the car refused to move. Lafi pushed it into a secondhand car lot and left it as down payment on another car. A visiting relative borrowed this one and wrecked it beyond repair. The lawyer's problem—how many cars could Lafi be charged for? God's problem—how could he pay for any of them?

Vai talked often of his family in Samoa, and I soon felt as if I knew them myself. He did not consider himself descended from the carefree inhabitants of a tropical island. His ancestors were the Vikings of the Pacific who covered more uncharted water in an open canoe than Columbus did in the *Santa Maria*. We read a book called *The Far Lands of Maui* and I decided that his forebears measured up quite well to my Pilgrims. Vai's idea of an ideal vacation was to build a Samoan double canoe and sail the southern seas. I was all for joining him until I discovered that his knowledge of navigation by no means measured up to that of his ancestors.

Vai's grandfather had been a wandering minstrel and lover of some repute in the villages. His songs were so impressive that he acquired twenty wives before the missionaries caught up with him.

Vai's father had an equally winsome personality but his first love was the church. He was one of the first Samoans to leave the islands for an outside education. In 1902 he went to a Methodist Church school in the Tongan islands, about five hundred miles south of Samoa. Tongan curriculum in those days relied heavily on Dante's *Inferno*. Ala'i's letters to Vai almost fifty years later were studded with references to "fallen angels" and "seven heavens."

But Dante apparently left Ala'i with room for thought. In his first letter to me, Ala'i asked what existed before the world began. Not being at all sure, I sent him a clipping about electrical particles and the expanding universe. In the next letter he wrote that he had explained this to his congregation but had been unable to locate the Biblical reference. At Vai's suggestion I sent him my mortarboard which he thereafter wore to church. He referred to it lovingly as "my square hat" and never has it graced a more deserving head.

Without Vai's mother, however, Ala'i would never have survived the practical problems of existence. Tupuasa was large and capable. She had to be. To his own fourteen, Ala'i added ten or twelve adopted children, as well as the young ladies of the village who were sent to him for training and protection. His home was also a hospital for the village sick.

It was with the sick that Tupuasa particularly excelled.

She was a master at the art of massage and had a thorough knowledge of Samoan medicinal plants. To this she added vast practical experience in midwifery and Christian consolation.

Tupuasa's mind was of the retentive rather than the inquisitive variety. It stored prodigious quantities of genealogical material. In the Library of Congress Vai and I found a book by Turner giving the genealogy of Samoan leading families for generations. Since Tupuasa belonged to one of these families Vai wrote her to send her version of the family tree. Her account varied from Turner's in only one name.

To me Vai was just as romantic as his ancestors. He might butch-cut his hair, speak cowboy English, wear slacks and sweaters—that was only a veneer. Underneath he was solid Samoan.

Night and day were the same to him. He was as apt to ask me for a stroll at 5 A.M. as at 7 P.M. I don't know whether it was the hour or the company but Washington seemed enchanted at that time of morning.

Mealtimes were equally a matter of indifference. Sometimes we had two feasts in a row. Sometimes he apparently did not eat for days. Once when thoughts of Samoa made him homesick Vai purchased three ancient coconuts with his last dollar. Scraped, squeezed, and baked with supermarket spinach, it was the nearest American approach to a favorite Samoan delicacy called *palusami*. It was not a very close approach but the process was so lovingly performed that I felt homesick myself.

Vai had an absolute genius for making dead parties come to life. At those excruciatingly formal functions where one is supposed to dangle a cocktail and agonize over what to say to the boss, Vai was apt to pull out his ukulele and burst into song. The party usually wound up with the boss joining a siva dance and everyone feeling that it was the most natural thing in the world.

Vai talked knowingly of American mechanical inventions without the slightest idea of what was involved. One weekend he proposed to visit my sister in New Jersey and my father kindly offered his new car for the trip. On the way Vai talked familiarly about models and horsepowers, cylinders and hydramatic drive. I gave him the wheel assuming I had met a master. I hadn't. Within five minutes we were entangled with the rear end of a bus which had dutifully stopped at a railway crossing. We limped home with a smashed radiator, an insurance suit, and an empty exchequer. It was a tribute to my father's unusual generosity and Vai's unusual charm that they continued to be on speaking terms.

Vai had not yet grasped the full implications of living in a monetary economy. His friends might have resented footing the bills so many times except for the disconcerting fact that Vai usually acquired the bills in an excess of good will towards those very friends. Early in November I left for Chicago to take my final exams. At 3 A.M. the night before the exam the telephone rang and I was treated to a full half hour of Samoan chanting long distance from Washington. I went to my exam walking on air and can't even recollect the questions. But my roommate can recollect to this day the phone bill that came in at the end of that month.

In matters of religion Vai felt more at home with my grandmother than with me. His letters to his father began with dutiful references to "the Glorious Three-in-one." I know he had a serious talk with his Methodist pastor about my untheological inclinations. Membership in the Samoan Methodist Church is based on rather strict notions regarding dancing, drinking, smoking, and picnicking on Sunday. It was obvious that neither Vai nor I could be in a state

of grace in Samoa for more than a few days at a time.
But the Samoan Church knew that it could never quite
tame the Samoan spirit. It was always ready to forgive and
try again. I had good cause to be thankful for the religious
training Ala'i had given his sons. Their deep loyalty to the
church gave them not only lodgings but something to tie
to in the States, and it proved to be the one area in which
his Polynesian family and my Puritan family spoke the
same language.

To Vai, America was simply a school. Samoa was home,
and he was restless to return. His twin ambitions were to
work for the Samoan Government and develop his family
land. In the olden days his forefathers had dominated the
tiny village of Salani on the south coast of Upolu. The
family still claimed a considerable tract of virgin rainforest
behind the village. His ancestors had a reputation for ruth-
lessness. But in recent times the more enterprising members
of the family had become pastors instead of chiefs. Many
of the great old titles remained unfilled. Salani had changed
from the proud home of Queen Salamasina to a sleepy
little clearing eight miles from the nearest road. Vai's
master's thesis was a study of how he would develop Salani
and its rich forest and ocean resources without destroying
its beloved Samoan way of life. He longed to make his
thesis an actual fact.

Before long Vai and I did reach the stage of discussing
Margaret Mead. Vai had never actually read *Coming of
Age in Samoa* but so many people had asked him about
it that he had definite opinions on its contents. He completely disagreed with the thesis that Samoan adolescence
was not a period of "Sturm und Drang." Respectable young
Samoan ladies at a critical age usually lived with the
village pastor for safekeeping, he told me. Any red-blooded
young Samoan considered it a challenge to his manhood to
make at least one nocturnal visit to the pastor's household.

This was a perilous undertaking since girls and guardians slept side by side in a one-roomed house or *fale* as they call it. At the slightest alarm the whole village would be up for the chase with bush knives. This custom provided plenty of *sturm und drang* even for adventurous souls like Vai. I suppose I should have been terrified of a young man with a background like that. But he described it all with such zest that I could feel nothing but admiration. Vai seemed to have inherited something directly from his grandfather. I only hoped it wasn't a yen for twenty wives.

The problems of bridging cultures never occurred to me. It wouldn't have made much difference anyhow. If Vai had been a purple man with fluorescent hair I would have accompanied him to Mars without a backward glance. I just couldn't help it.

Vai never did ask me to marry him. I guess he just assumed I would. But my mother took nothing for granted. She wanted to know.

I shall not soon forget our family Thanksgiving dinner in 1951. My family was very fond of Vai and had carefully informed him of proper procedures in American custom. My mother prepared a feast worthy of the Pilgrims. Vai himself was in great form, as if he had asked for daughters' hands in marriage on any number of previous occasions. I felt like an innocent bystander. Only my father was nervous. He had weathered two similar crises with my sisters, but he never seemed to get over the fear that he would unwittingly say something wrong and leave one of his daughters a spinster for life.

When we were well along on the turkey Vai casually stated with a grin that he and I would like to be married. My father stammered. My mother said, "When?" The family decided on January twenty-fifth and that was that.

We went to the District Building in Washington for our

license. The application did not request information as to Vai's race but it did want to know his color.

I looked him over critically. It was a nice color, I decided, light brown with some red in it. "Copper" was the only word for it and I filled in the application accordingly. We passed our forms to the secretary and sat down. After several minutes there was a commotion behind the rail.

"Which one of you is 'copper' colored?" the secretary called out to the prospective husbands. They looked at each other in some surprise. They covered quite a range of colors, but no one moved.

"You look about like that," I whispered to Vai defensively.

"If you think so, you go up and tell her," he whispered angrily. I did.

"People just can't be that color," the secretary told me flatly.

"Well, what would you call him?" I asked, pointing to Vai.

She looked at him curiously.

"Tan," she decided finally, and we got married on that.

From the point of view of my family's exchequer and talents a Samoan wedding was out of the question.

"You can have another wedding when you get to Samoa," Mother told Vai firmly. "We will stick to something I can cope with."

The result was simple but satisfying. The sixty or seventy wedding guests included relatives, labor leaders, Samoans, the New Zealand consul, the staff of Vai's office, and the governor of American Samoa, who had flown in for budget hearings.

My sisters and their husbands were determined to make our getaway an experience to be remembered. They had planned for everything, cans, stalled cars, old shoes, tooting horns, and placards. What they had not reckoned on was the enchantment of Samoan entertainment. My sisters as well as the guests got so involved in sivas and war chants that Vai and I chugged peacefully off to Washington in my father's car.

My parents had invited us to live with them until our theses were complete. So they thoughtfully spent our honeymoon in Florida while Vai and I returned next day to a house thoroughly scrambled by my vengeful sisters. The ensuing honeymoon was worthy of my Puritan ancestors. I had to spend it writing Vai's thesis to meet an inconvenient deadline.

This domestic arrangement was, I hasten to say, with the full consent of his professors. They had been experiencing considerable difficulty understanding what he had written, and they thought he needed an English editor. I soon discovered that English wasn't the problem at all. It was Samoan custom itself that was incomprehensible.

With a stretch of the imagination I could conceive of four simultaneous paramount chiefs, but it took me several days to grasp the idea that a chief dropped his baptismal name and was referred to only by his title. If a chief had five titles he had five different names in five different villages. Titular hierarchies might be expected to lead to one paramount chief or another—but they didn't—they led to several. The paramounts might have simplified things by ruling one island each—but no—their villages were interspersed through all the islands. Most families claimed a relationship to several titles. I could understand one ordinary chief ruling one family until I found that titles were infinitely divisible. There were, for example, sixteen simultaneous incumbents of the Fuima title in Vai's village of Salani. By the time all this was committed to paper the professor could not understand my English either.

But American University took it on faith. Vai got his master's degree.

CHAPTER THREE

Return of the Native

Living with in-laws was no problem to Vai. Everyone does it in Samoa. And living with Vai was no problem to my parents. He gave a great boost to family morale. He was sometimes a problem to mine, however. I must admit it ruffled me to observe him calmly enjoying a chess game with my sister while I sweated over his thesis.

But despite Vai's attachment to my family and his office, he grew increasingly restless to return to Samoa. After mastering his thesis I was somewhat curious myself to see four paramount chiefs in action.

Early next spring we both sent employment applications to the government of Western Samoa. Western Samoa was a trust territory of New Zealand and included the island of Savaii where Vai was born and the island of Upolu where Apia, the capital, and Salani, Vai's village, were located. Vai hoped to work for the government and in his spare time try out his thesis on Salani.

Since he was the only full Samoan with a master's degree, and since Western Samoa was his home, it was a blow to discover that the government could not use either of us. Vai was angry and disconsolate by turns, but he still wanted to go home.

A few of the smaller islands of Samoa are a non-self-governing territory of the United States. So we turned to the United States Department of the Interior, and this time had better results. Vai was appointed assistant personnel officer for American Samoa. A young Samoan lawyer who had been our best man was made public defender about the same time. Pete and Vai were the first Samoans to return with graduate degrees, thanks to the GI Bill of Rights.

The two of them presented the government with some new problems, however. Should they be given the salaries they had been earning in the States, or should these be reduced to one half in line with the Samoan economy? Should they be granted return transportation like other stateside personnel? Should they be asked to join the island club? There seemed to be no clear answer to such questions.

Packing for the trip was complicated by the fact that I was expecting to add one new little Samoan to the islands shortly after arrival and felt I should be equipped with crib, tub, and high chair. We also seemed to be carrying not only our own things but those of numerous relatives. Lafi, for example, contributed several of his sixteen pieces of luggage full of clothes for folks back home. We carried material for sixty lavalavas, a gown to go with Ala'i's "square hat," and a flush toilet for "Grandma." I wondered at the time whether Samoan houses had running water and where they located sanitary facilities in a house with no sides, but my concern was wasted. Later I discovered that toilets were a matter of prestige rather than convenience at least to "Grandma." This one was never attached to anything.

The Department of the Interior kindly provided us the honeymoon that the thesis had denied. It assigned Vai to understudy the Hawaiian personnel system before proceeding to American Samoa. We spent one idyllic month near Waikiki in a little apartment with a patio. We visited Vai's old teachers, and became festively involved with the Samoan community.

Hawaiians may be on the verge of extinction in Hawaii, but Samoans certainly are not. After World War II the United States forces recruited several hundred young Samoans and stationed them in Hawaii. The year before our arrival the Navy had offered to bring over the dependents of these men. But the Navy had forgotten to check into the number this would involve. Most Samoans are related to each other, few are financially independent, and all love to travel. The SS *President Jackson* which went to fetch several hundred dependents returned with several thousand, some still in lavalavas and bare feet. The housing problem didn't worry the immigrants; they simply moved in with their Samoan relatives. But Hawaiian social workers felt that six or eight to a room was overcrowding. A number of the arriving Samoans had never worked for wages before and didn't seem particularly anxious to begin.

But economic considerations never inhibit Samoan hospitality. We were warmly welcomed and I was soon introduced to baked breadfruit, the genuine version of palusami, raw fish, and taro. I can't say that I was converted to boiled green bananas, however, despite my later close association with them.

Vai was determined to get to Samoa for Christmas, so, by the middle of December we were on our way again. It was the hot, damp season in the tropics. Stepping off the plane at Fiji felt like opening the door of a hothouse.

By the time we reached Samoa, however, I was beyond noticing the weather. From our flying boat the island of Upolu looked like a cluster of coconut trees adrift on the ocean.

Father Ala'i had given strict orders that we were to be introduced to the family, not at the airport, but in his church. So we were met only by a one-eyed uncle and his wife who presented me with a large cake.

After a considerable wait for our luggage, we squeezed

into a little car and sputtered off—not to Apia, Samoa's only town, but towards the tiny village of Salamumu across the central mountain range, where the family was waiting for us.

Evening was falling as we passed through the little thatched villages along the north coast. Everyone was out for a twilight stroll. Some were draped in bed sheets, and looked like ghosts in the gathering shadows. Others were seated casually in the middle of the road chatting with their friends. The assembly had passed a law against sleeping in the road, but the warmth of the sun seemed to linger there, and it was still a temptation.

Kerosene lamps on the floor of every fale twinkled like stars through the breadfruit leaves. These fales consisted of little round thatched roofs on poles. Not only were there no sides to the houses, but almost no furniture. The effect was simple and enchanting.

Before long we turned inland and climbed upwards into a forest. Heavy creepers fell from the trees like giant snakes. Ferns the size of trees hung gracefully over the car, and plants with leaves as big as table cloths brushed against the window. As we started down the other side of the range everyone kept an eye out for the turnoff to Salamumu.

I could have lost that road while sitting on it. It was just two overgrown tracks through the trees. Weeds scraped the bottom of the car as we plunged forward. Nevertheless that road represented considerable labor. In an effort to attach themselves to the main road, Salamumu villagers had lugged tons of coral sand to lay this track across the marshes.

After three rough miles we heard the roar of the surf and suddenly emerged onto a long strand of smooth white sand gleaming in the moonlight. On our right curled the long white breakers of the Pacific. On our left slumbered a long single line of thatched houses, each with its little kitchen fale and outdoor oven behind. Here and there the ruddy

vasiliu

glow of a heating oven pit played on the low-hanging bread-fruit trees. I couldn't believe it was real.

The car headed straight for the church, which was the only western-style structure in the village. It was hard to tell whether this church was in the process of construction or destruction. It was simply four cement walls with holes where window frames had obviously never rested. The kerosene lighted interior, I saw as we entered, was devoid of furnishings except for a table and two enormous chairs up in front. The congregation sat cross-legged on mats on the floor.

To my dismay every eye was turned not forwards towards the table but backwards towards me. I endeavored to sink quietly onto a mat by the door, but was politely pushed forward with Vai towards the two chairs in the front. All eyes moved with us. From just outside broke the eerie percussion of a hollow log drum. Suddenly everything seemed incredibly strange. What was I doing here? I turned to run, but Vai reached for my hand.

As soon as we were seated and I found enough courage to look at the congregation I discovered that they were quite peaceable. They had apparently been awaiting our arrival for some time. Father Ala'i, enveloped in a long black robe and my "square hat," now swept forward to the table. He was shorter than Vai, but with an utterly relaxed and beatific countenance. He never glanced once at us. When he reached the table he cast up his eyes with a sublime smile and started a song.

I had expected music somewhat in line with the architecture and was utterly astonished. The congregation sounded like a great organ—rich, vibrant, and confident. Bass voices played a complicated fugue below and sopranos soared above. Everyone sang. Obviously they were not new to this sort of thing. The music restored my confidence. I even stumbled along on the Samoan scripture reading which came next. Towards the end it suddenly dawned on me that we were reading our old familiar family psalm:

But the mercy of the Lord is from everlasting to everlasting upon them that fear him, and his righteousness unto childrens' children.

Separated by an ocean and a culture, Vai's family and mine were one in these words. Perhaps it was not so strange after all for my Scotch-Irish name to appear in the fifty-fourth generation of Tupuasa's Samoan genealogy.

With a whisper and a nod Vai indicated his mother sitting on the floor beside the table. She was twice the size of Ala'i, lengthwise and crosswise, and the effect was not diminished by a white sateen dress and enormous straw hat. She seemed to be as conscious of this world as Ala'i was of the next and was busily engaged in keeping her numerous grandchildren awake and upright by sharp raps of a palm leaf fan. Four of Vai's five sisters were present. Fetu's face reflected the quiet beauty of her father, and Taligi had the masculine strength and size of her mother. The other two bustled confidently in and out. I decided I could never afford to argue with the maternal side of my in-laws.

Ala'i began a prayer and the congregation tipped forward on the mats, faces in hands, rear ends in the air. It was a half-hour prayer covering my meeting with Vai, our marriage, and the Christian characteristics of each member of my family. The village was apparently on a first-name basis with all my relatives. When the prayer was over a few members of the congregation did not resume a sitting position. Apparently they had fallen asleep. This did not disconcert Ala'i in the least. He passed the collection plate and to my great embarrassment presented the contents to me. I made a short speech in English about windows for the church and presented it back to him again.

After the service Vai's mother called out the names of the family and they came up to kiss us one by one. I had no idea I was related to so many people. After twenty minutes I was sure I must have kissed everyone in the village and some twice.

We walked across the small yard to the parsonage. It was a beautiful example of a Samoan fale. Six heavy interior posts inside a circle of smaller posts held up the large thatched dome. I couldn't take my eyes off the under side of the roof. What at first seemed to be carving proved to be intricate lashings tying the thatch to delicate poles. The floor was of waterworn coral covered with thick pandanus mats. Every post was woven over with leaves and flowers to celebrate our homecoming and garlands of hibiscus formed a ceiling. In the soft kerosene light it was enchanting. I could see busy preparations in the cookhouse behind.

Inside the fale the chiefs arranged themselves cross-legged, each at a post. Tupuasa and Ala'i sat at the head of the circle. Vai, though not a chief, was honored guest, so we sat at the foot. I recalled painfully that sitting tailor-fashion was recommended for expectant mothers, and smiled dutifully. For a few minutes everyone chatted and laughed and slapped his thighs jovially. Suddenly a young man appeared with a long, gnarled stick, scraped white. The fale quieted. Handling the root pensively, an old chief made a solemn speech presenting it to Vai. The kava ceremony had begun. A young girl flanked by two young men seated herself behind a four-legged wooden bowl at the back of the house. One of the boys shook a leaf of pounded kava root into the bowl, another ladled in water with half a coconut shell. The girl kneaded and squeezed the liquid with a roll of fiber. Her motions were as sure and graceful as a dancer's. At intervals she tossed the fiber strainer to a young man outside who shook it out and tossed it back. Gradually the liquid took on a brownish hue. She held up the strainer and let it drip back into the bowl. The chiefs nodded approval. The Village Virgin—leading maiden of the village and daughter of a chief—had made well the ancient ceremonial drink of the Samoans.

The chiefs clapped their hands. One let out a fearsome shout followed by a volley of words. A young man jumped up, scooped up a coconut shell of kava, lifted it above his head and strode to the middle of the circle. The chief shouted again; the young man turned slowly and with a couple of steps and a sweep of the arm handed it to the village pastor. Men of God are always served first in Ala'i's household. Vai was served second. To come next after the pastor was a great honor, especially to a young man who was not even a chief. Vai had never sat with the *matai* (family chiefs) before and was so overwhelmed that the proper ceremonial reply slipped his mind. A talking chief, who in Samoa is a speechmaker and authority on protocol, came to his rescue. Vai poured out a drop to the gods and drank, tossing the dregs over his shoulder.

After him the chiefs were served in turn according to their rank in the village hierarchy.

When the ceremony was over a line of chanting figures crossed the sand towards us in the moonlight. First in line was the Village Maiden, the sticks of her headdress protruding like horns from an unruly wig of orange hair. Behind her came a woman carrying a large, fine mat folded in half. Ladies with tapa cloths followed. This was the gift-giving ceremony.

The fine mat was swept gracefully around the circle before the guests who whispered words of respect as it passed. Woven with infinite patience from pandanus leaves split fine as threads, and bordered with red feathers, these incredibly soft and pliable fine mats are the ceremonial currency of Samoa. They have no apparent practical use, and some of the most famous mats are full of holes, but the dignity of any occasion is measured by the number and history of the fine mats exchanged. This particular mat was called a royal fine mat because it had been woven by a great-aunt on the occasion of her marriage into one of the royal lines. It had helped determine family history and was held in high esteem. The aunt had printed her name in the corner.

The important chiefs accompanied these gifts with long speeches of welcome during which Vai muttered "*malie* [nice]" and "*fa'afetai* [thank you]." Then, since much of the speaking seemed to be addressed to me, I volunteered a two-minute speech in English. Vai whispered urgently that I had made a serious ceremonial mistake. Our talking chief was supposed to say thank you for us. The talking chief was so obviously disappointed that I hastily asked him to translate. The translation took twenty minutes so I am sure he must have said the right things.

After the presents came the feast. Four young men came across the sand carrying a bier upon which lay an enormous roast pig with flowers in his ears. A girl appeared with a pierced coconut, then others with leaf trays of taro, chicken, salt beef, and palusami. These we ate with speed and in silence in deference to the talking chiefs who were supposed to wait until we were through. But we had no sooner finished than a group of young men arrived with baskets of canned meat, taro, and bundles of fish. At the doorstep they handed their baskets to a chief who opened them and shouted out the contents and the name of the donor in a voice which must have aroused the entire village. I discovered later that formal gifts of food are always acknowledged in this fashion. It was well past midnight now and we had just finished one meal, but no one objected to this second array. In fact everyone seemed delighted. The food had made a mountain in the middle of the floor. But under the direction of a talking chief it vanished as quickly as it had appeared. As far as I could determine he had divided it among the very people who brought it. The children ran off happily with their coconut baskets full of food. In a few minutes the entire village was participating in our welcome feast.

Shortly thereafter I discovered that my crossed legs were painfully asleep. I was practically asleep myself for that matter. My sisters-in-law sensed my problem. They pulled down a mattress from the rafters, hung up a mosquito net, and draped a curtain across one end of the fale. I bowed sleepily to the chiefs and retired. Undressing was an insurmountable problem. The curtain screened me from the matai but there was nothing between me and the children outside. I finally went to bed as I was. But not to sleep. I was a novice with mosquito nets, and an ignoramus when it came to the little singing products of the Salamumu marshes. No matter how carefully I tucked myself in I felt as if I had been set on fire. I took a look at their striped legs. They looked like anopheles. I buried myself head and all under the sheet. It did no good. Eventually my sisters-in-law heard my groans. They shook the net vigorously. Out poured thousands of the little monsters. The girls quickly tucked me in again. I still burned, but I went to sleep.

When I awoke next morning the chiefs had gone, but Vai and the family were still in the same position on the floor. They had talked all night.

Today, they informed me, was my wedding day. I glanced meaningfully at my eight-months pregnant figure but apparently they did not find it in the least incongruous.

Preparations for the day were well under way already. A canopy of coconut leaves had been erected on the poles in front of the house. Banana leaves were spread beneath for a table. An oven (umu) of hot rocks steamed in the back yard.

Sister Fetu was cranking an ancient sewing machine on

the floor at the back of the fale and shortly presented me with a lavalava and smock which had the double advantage of fitting a form like mine and being changeable in public. One merely knotted a clean lavalava around the waist and dropped the used one. As open fales seemed to necessitate such clothing I gratefully accepted. I do confess to some insecurity about keeping it up with the customary Samoan twist. I anchored mine with safety pins.

A drum made of a hollow log sounded and we stepped out of the house and into the church for our second wedding.

After church the chiefs resumed their posts and the ceremonies of the previous evening started again; the kava, the gifts, the food. Last night was a welcome, this was a wedding. How the little village of Salamumu, stranded on a strip of sand between swamp and ocean, could afford two such displays in a row I could not understand. But no one seemed dismayed.

Samoan weddings usually involve a vast exchange of gifts between the girl's and the boy's families. If the couple receive anything personally it is merely incidental. The girl's family usually present craftwork, and the boy's family food and money. Canny talking chiefs calculate the balance. The side that presents most is victorious. The winning family may be bankrupt, but its prestige is enormous and that is what counts.

Our Samoan wedding was complicated by the fact that relatives from my side were not present. In any case, my mother does not know how to make fine mats, and my family couldn't begin to afford such a display of wealth. Vai's family graciously offered to take both sides of the occasion. They outdid themselves, tapas, bed mats, woven baskets, shells, beads, tortoise shell and silver jewelry, a duster made of bird of paradise feathers from New Guinea, and pins made from toothbrush handles. The social importance of a wedding, however, is really determined by the number of fine mats involved. We rated eight. Each one was spread out, admired, and swept around the house over the heads of the guests. A talking chief then began the division. In typical fashion Ala'i felt the fine mats should be given to the village pastor. The latter felt this was too much. He returned three. Two of these Vai and I were supposed to use as payment on the occasion of his future tattooing. As far as I was concerned that would be a long time. The other was to be for our daughter's wedding, providing we had a girl. I was grateful for that since I am no more adept at making fine mats than my mother is.

As the rest of the things were being distributed among relatives and dignitaries my eye rested on an enormous tapa cloth at least twelve feet in length by ten feet in width. It was a beautiful thing. My mother-in-law had beaten the cloth herself from the bark of the mulberry tree and had painted it with geometric wheels of black, brown, yellow, and green stains collected from lamp soot, roots, bark, and berries. I could see it as a family heirloom and boldly staked a claim. It is unpardonable for a bride to claim one of the wedding gifts but I discovered right then the advantage of being an ignorant foreigner. If there is one thing Samoans prize higher than custom it is politeness to strangers. I was graciously presented with the tapa.

After the gifts came the feast which outdid the previous evening's by quite a margin. The table was shaped like a T and extended halfway across the village square. A talking chief called out the names and well over a hundred guests sat down on the mats. Each guest stationed a child with a basket behind him, and with good reason. As soon as the prayer was over there was a great commotion as guests tossed taros, lobsters, chickens, whole cakes, and plates of salad into their baskets. The table was dismantled in a twinkling. Very little food was consumed on location, so that

Vasiliu

the feast could be appreciated not only by the guests but by all the relatives of the guests. I was just thankful that I hadn't provided the guests with baskets at Lusi's welcome feast back in Washington.

Vai and I sat at the head of the table screened by a wedding cake nine stories high. I imagined the cake must contain a frosted box or two, but no, it was solid fruit cake from top to bottom. The cake was surmounted with two candles. At the proper moment Vai blew out one and I blew out the other. Starting with the top layer for the pastor, I was supposed to divide it fairly among 280 villagers. Only a talking chief could do that. Fortunately a thunderstorm broke just as I started. It blew down the leaf house, began to dissolve the frosting, and left a puddle in the middle of the cake before we could rush it into the fale.

Upon completion of this feast I felt thoroughly married and also in need of exercise. It seemed a logical moment to take a walk around the village by myself. I had not counted on the retinue that immediately appeared. One can find solitude in the Chicago Loop, but not in Samoa. Any move of mine was accompanied by every child and dog in the village. But white sand, gay flowers, and dappled sunlight under the palms urged me to explore. The warm, brilliant day seemed like anything but December 24.

Salamumu's commercial district consisted of a one-room shack where one could exchange sun-dried copra or cocoa beans for well-aged tins of corned beef or herrings. Business was not brisk. Life was quite possible without canned fish.

Salamumu's water system was unique. Housewives turned neither to a pipe nor a well. They simply dug a hole in the sand. This filled miraculously, not with brine, but with fresh water seeping down from the mountains. They washed their clothes by a rock in the sea where the water welled up fresh from an underwater spring.

Sanitary facilities were equally simple. The only latrine

in town was owned, fortunately, by my father-in-law. He had provided it for the convenience of visiting missionaries. But it certainly did not add to the beauty of Salamumu. It was a dilapidated little shack built of packing-case boards and perched precariously on sticks at low tide mark right in front of the pastor's house. Ordinarily it was kept locked but European visitors were graciously presented with the key. Everyone else resorted to a picturesque portion of the beach where one could sit on the white sand and enjoy an unrivaled view of the blue Pacific from under the shade of the overhanging palms, and where nature herself did an exceptional job of scouring twice a day with the swirling tide.

I couldn't locate the school at all. Apparently it was indistinguishable from the rest of the fales, and besides, all the pupils were with me.

The churches were obvious enough. Salamumu's thirty families could choose either (or both) the Methodist and the London Missionary Society. Each had a substantial but unfinished edifice. Vai had told me that other villages nearby had the added option of Catholic and Mormon churches. Samoa seemed to provide for everyone but atheists.

I got back to Ala'i's fale to discover a siva dance in progress. Dancing is permissible to Methodists before 5 P.M., and the crowd, packed closely around the house, was making the most of it. Inside, a group of garlanded girls swayed gracefully to the twang of a guitar, three ukuleles, and a double bass made by snapping a string held taut by a stick braced on top of a kerosene drum. A chorus provided the melody. A group of boys on one side of the house was taking turns at entertainment with a group of girls on the other. After the girls finished dancing the boys produced a dramatic story in song about how Vai went to the States and found me. I didn't dare ask for details but it caused great hilarity. Then the girls did a sitting dance with snapping sticks.

Vai was not in evidence at all. He had always refused to dance for me and I had presumed this was one bit of Samoan culture that had passed him by. To my amazement he appeared for the next number. I scarcely recognized him. From shoulder to toe his smooth brown body glistened with perfumed coconut oil. Across his face was a fierce black smear. A double red hibiscus graced his ear and shiny brown nuts clacked on his ankles. His only other adornment was a short skirt of shiny green leaves.

When he began to dance it seemed like rhythm devoid of motion; a set of the head, a flick of the wrist, an imperceptible undulation of the knees, everything in perfect balance. I couldn't believe that dancing could be so delicate and yet so masculine. The pace accelerated with the music but never into violent motion. If only more wives could see their husbands dance like that!

Someone indicated that it was now appropriate for me to join Vai. A slender Samoan maiden would no doubt have provided a fitting climax to the occasion, but in my present shape I felt that I couldn't defile the grace of the moment.

As dusk fell, the drum sounded and everyone retired for family prayers. I could hear hymns rising from every fale in the village but Ala'i's were loudest and longest of all, as befits a pastor. After this we had a more informal visit from the matai. After consuming a gluey but delicious mixture of starch and coconut cream, they began joking about the wives who had been brought back to the village. Fala went to Fiji and came home with a black one. Vai went to America and came home with a white one. Noa went to New Guinea and came back with three! The chiefs particularly wanted to see our diplomas and caps and gowns. Some of the matai were from Ala'i's family in Salani and Vai soon embarked on his favorite subject, how to develop that village without destroying its Samoanness. He produced a copy of our thesis. The advantage of this masterpiece was that it was safe anywhere. The professors who passed it in Washington didn't know enough about Samoan custom to criticize it. The Samoans who did, couldn't read it. But they were impressed with the typing and the diagrams and were soon in an animated discussion of piped water, co-op stores, and even hydroelectric power.

Vai again spent the night in conversation while I retired. The girls beat the bed, fanned the air, and shook the netting. Someone passed in an ancient can of Flit. I jumped inside and the girls tied everything down securely. It worked. I was soon asleep.

In the middle of the night I vaguely heard the drum beating again. Suddenly there was a burst of song nearby that roused me with a start. Didn't these people ever sleep!

It seemed incredible that this balmy night was Christmas Eve. The fale was surrounded with carolers. We dressed and went to church for a midnight service. The hymns were different but the scriptures were the same. Vai and I staggered to bed at 5 A.M. The drum sounded for church again at six but fortunately Vai never heard it. I didn't move either. After all there was another service at nine o'clock.

Christmas presents are as unheard of in Samoa as chimneys and stockings but I can't say I was disappointed. Any further outlay would certainly have embarrassed both me and the village.

Between Christmas and New Year's, Apia closes down. No boats were sailing for American Samoa. Vai had been scheduled to start work on December 27. Finally we wired the governor. I am not sure whether that gentleman was concerned about us or the mail, but he did send a boat.

The family gathered again to see us off. Considering the tears and flowers, one would have thought we were leaving

for Africa instead of the next island. Many of them wanted
to go with us but I explained firmly that the number of
people we could afford to support on Vai's income was
more limited than it had been in America. When the little
boat finally cast off we were accompanied only by a pretty
little cousin who happened to be a nurse.

It is said that the unusual motion of the MV *Samoa* is
due to the fact that its two propellers both screw in the
same direction. This particular night its native bent was
accentuated by a headwind and enormous waves which
smacked into us as soon as we crossed the reef. Our little
cousin succumbed first. That boat didn't just go up and
down. It stood on its head. Most of the time the waves
seemed to be above us rather than below and when they
broke only a rigged-up canvas separated the fifty bodies
entangled on the hatch cover from the deluge. I would
probably have produced our baby on the spot had I not
been rigid with fright.

Sixty miles and an eternity later we staggered into the
delicious calm of Pago Pago Harbor. It was 3 A.M. and the
moon suddenly burst from the clouds over Rainmaker
Mountain above us. No matter how small and steep this
little rock in the Pacific might prove, I was prepared to
stick by it for life.

CHAPTER FOUR

Seven Samoan Sons

I thought I had been introduced to all my Samoan relatives at Salamumu, but I found I had barely begun. Shortly after we arrived in Tutuila and succeeded in squeezing our boxes and the crated toilet through the door of our little frame house, Vai said, "Now it's time to pay our respects to Grandma."

Sure enough, I hadn't met Grandmother. Hand in hand we strolled down the road, past a row of roomy verandahed houses.

"This," Vai informed me, "is Centipede Row, where the higher government officials live. I helped build these houses when I worked for the Navy. This one at the end is where the Captain of the Yard used to live."

We passed the wharf and post office, crossed the village green which was surrounded with wooden stores, and turned into a stony little alley up the mountainside. We had crossed the entire town at a leisurely pace in less than fifteen minutes. The Samoan community on the slope above the stores was a crowded hodge-podge of half-breed houses: tin and thatch, shacks and fales, water pipes and umus, all mixed together in a most cosmopolitan fashion.

Grandma's house was no exception. Squeezed tightly between a rough plank church and three board shacks, it was
composed, Samoan fashion, of a single platform surrounded
by round posts. But it had collected some Western features
as well. The floor was made of packing-case boards and
the roof of tin. The floor was elevated three or four feet
above the ground which gave it a two-story effect. Grandma
was taking a siesta on a mat under the house when we
arrived.

Like Tupuasa, her daughter, Grandma had once been an
impressively sized woman. But her legs now resented their
burden and she spent most of her days seated like a many-
layered triangular Buddha under the house. Her face had
its full eighty-year share of creases and wrinkles and her
eyes were almost sightless. But the total effect somehow
was one of great dignity and repose. She looked and acted
like the descendant of Samoan kings, as indeed she was.

Everyone treated her with the greatest respect, and it
soon became apparent who had final word in the household. Here she was undoubtedly matai. The size of the
household took me aback. Lua, Grandma's youngest daughter, still unmarried, was chief cook, laundress, sergeant, and
supply officer. Fortunately God had blessed Lua with a
sturdy body and a sturdier tongue, since she performed
these essential services for grandson Iakopo, his wife and
four children, adopted grandson Iosua, his wife and three
children, and seven miscellaneous adolescents whom Ala'i
had sent to Tutuila for an education. Somehow they all
lived on or under this 15-by-30-foot platform with one
electric light, no running water, no toilet, no stove, and
no visible means of support. The economics of this arrangement troubled me. But by now I too was beginning
to believe God had made special provision for Samoans.
The family had evidently been getting along like this quite
happily for some time. They certainly did not consider

themselves poor, and the welcome feast they spread before us in the schoolhouse nearby indicated no hardship.

Next morning Lua appeared at my house. She had come, she told me, to be our housegirl, and she would gladly work without pay since we were all relatives. I was astonished at this offer, knowing her responsibilities at home. I called Vai for advice.

"Oh, we must have Lua," he said. "She helped raise me and she can help raise my children."

So I agreed to the arrangement, insisting on paying the prevailing wage for housegirls, which wasn't much. I also agreed to send meals up for Grandma. That was the least I could do in return for taking her chief sergeant.

At the conclusion of our first meal I began to wonder if perhaps God might be calling on me to help perform one of His Samoan miracles. By the end of the first week I was sure of it. Grandma apparently had an enormous appetite. She consumed a kettle of oatmeal, a full loaf of bread, half a pound of butter, several pots of coffee, and a dozen ripe bananas for breakfast. For lunch she needed ten hands of boiled green bananas. Supper was not conceivable without fifteen pounds of taro, a kettle of tea, and five pounds of herrings or corned beef. Grandma preferred her cakes and pies whole. She also had long repressed desires for mirrors, scissors, sheets, and dishes. It wasn't until I had hunted for these things for weeks that I realized the extent of Grandma's hardware needs.

Finally I followed a substantial meal to Grandma's house one day and found that it was being enjoyed not only by Grandma, the grandchildren, the great grandchildren, and the seven students, but also by the pastor and his wife and a few visitors. I was informed that no good Samoan could eat without sharing. Knowing how good a Samoan Grandma was, I was concerned. I called Vai into a stormy session at home. Unadvisedly I used the word "stealing" in connection with my hardware. Vai promptly set me straight. Stealing, I learned, was a Western term and was never to be used in connection with a Samoan, particularly Samoan relatives. Property, mine included, belonged to the entire family. If I couldn't bring myself to feel in a tribal way about things we would have to return to the States and live as individuals. I suggested more humbly that perhaps in deference to my American background, members of the family might ask first before "borrowing" my things. I found even this would imply possession. As the full implication of the Samoan concept of property dawned upon me, I suddenly realized why fales were practically devoid of furnishings. It would hardly pay one to surround himself with material possessions if these were at the disposal of any passing relative. I began to realize also why Samoans did not overwork themselves producing things. More food resulted simply in more visitors. As the wife of the only wage-earning member in the entire family I began to feel uneasy. Life in Samoa might not turn out to be as simple an idyl as it first appeared.

Unfortunately for me and the relatives, Vai was on a Samoan salary, just half of what he had been earning in the States. Unfortunately also, goods in the stores were more expensive than at home. While I might agree to a Samoan economic system, I couldn't, for the life of me, make it work. My poor Western mind was limited to the concept that somewhere, sometime, credits must equal debits. Since I couldn't shed my relatives so long as I stayed in Samoa, the only alternative was to make these relatives more productive.

That turned out to be difficult too. Iosua couldn't work because he was studying agriculture. Iakopo couldn't work because he had never acquired the habit. Lua was already working for everybody. None of the wives could work because we were all pregnant. The seven adolescents couldn't work because they were in school. The great grandchildren couldn't work because they were too young. Grandma couldn't move. Productive prospects seemed depressing.

Eventually at a stern family conclave Vai laid down a program. Lua was to work for another family and support Grandma from her earnings. Iosua was to continue agriculture school and support his family on the GI Bill. We would give Iakopo forty dollars a month until he could find employment. The seven students would come to live with us but would be expected to spend their free hours building a plantation on the mountaintop. The plantation would provide taro and bananas for everyone. With the exception of the arrangement for Iakopo, I heartily agreed.

I was suddenly called away from all this productive planning one night with the arrival of an even closer relative— a daughter of my own. Gloria was born at Pago Hospital under the kindly supervision of a Latvian doctor who had somehow found his way to this corner of the world.

The hospital was a medium-sized but well equipped gift of the American Navy, much like one I might have had at home. But the nurses were unique. In addition to routine maternity services they provided several hours a day of Samoan song, sitting casually on the end of the bed, rocking the baby on a practiced knee. The food was also unique. My first meal consisted of boiled rice, ungarnished macaroni, a piece of taro, and a thoughtfully added boiled potato.

To my relief we also developed a rooming-in system. One midnight at feeding time I was awakened by my daughter's howls of rage from the nursery on the floor below. After an hour I could stand it no longer. I padded down to see what was the matter. No one was around so I picked up my infant and brought her back upstairs with me. When she felt better I fixed her up comfortably in a bureau drawer and shoved her under the bed. There she remained. It was not until the next afternoon that someone missed her. By that time we were both irrevocably attached to the rooming-in plan.

When I returned home with my daughter I found that I had also acquired seven Samoan sons. Tala, Tapu, Pati, and Pita were Vai's real younger brothers. Pisa, Losi and Falevalu each had parents of their own but had been "adopted" by Ala'i and forwarded to Tutuila for an education. Their parents shared Ala'i's faith that God would provide. I never heard a word from them until graduation when they asked me to pay the boys' fares home.

Even Mrs. Dionne's family had not increased this rapidly and my seven older children, unfortunately, arrived with preconceived notions about life. I was uneasy about the whole affair, but not Vai. He finally felt like a matai.

The first thing obviously was to apply for a larger house. The government obligingly assigned us a place on the mountain directly above the police station. It was composed almost entirely of verandah.

I must confess to a feeling of maternal pride as I glanced around our large dinner table the first evening. All seven boys were stalwart, bronzed youths well on their way to six feet of Polynesian beauty. I could picture them singing as they carried great loads of our bananas down the mountainside. It was a bit strange to be called "Momma" by Pisa who was barely five years my junior, but then it was nice to come by a full-grown family with so little effort.

Vai felt we should set to work at once on their table manners since the boys were mistaking napkins for handkerchiefs. He gave such a stern lecture on forks versus fingers that the boys picked at their meat loaf like little birds and had to make up for it in the kitchen later. We never did conquer the boardinghouse reach. By the end of the first week, to the great relief of everyone concerned, we decided that the boys should eat in the kitchen except for Sunday dinner.

Beds were no problem. Our new sons just unrolled their mats on the porch, threw down a pillow, and rolled up in their lavalavas. But food was not so simple.

Pending bananas from the plantation I suggested pancakes for breakfast. Pati proceeded to produce not flabby circles, but fine, fat fritters in enormous quantities. When I inquired about the third dishpan full, he informed me that he was now working on their school lunch, which, according to Samoan custom, must be shared with their friends. He was not without friends. Breakfast and lunch the first day entailed ten pounds of flour and four pounds of drippings.

Pati continued to show an interest in cooking. In the evenings he made a sort of stew of meat, pumpkin, and flour. His previous experience with stews had been confined to open fires behind Samoan fales, but he soon mastered the art of turning on our electric stove. Unfortunately he never mastered the art of turning it off. Occasionally we discovered the stove a cheerful cherry red at midnight. Otherwise we found it well preheated for pancakes next morning.

Another Western invention that intrigued Pati was my pressure cooker. This pot, I warned him, was quick but dangerous and was to be used only under my supervision. Pati was unmoved. Seated one evening in the dining room, Vai and I heard a tremendous explosion. We rushed to the kitchen. Steaming stew was dripping from the ceiling. Falevalu was standing speechless in the center of the kitchen, his startled expression emphasized by the loss of both eyebrows. Pati had vanished completely.

We discovered him next morning at the hospital being treated for burns. He did not return for a week and showed no further interest in cooking.

A distinct advantage of Samoan sons is that they wear lavalavas instead of pants. Lavalavas being no more than a strip of cloth four feet long, nothing could be easier to

make, wash, or mend. Furthermore, Samoans wear no shoes. It was with concern therefore that I began to notice an increasing inclination towards Western dress.

It began with the mysterious disappearance of bottle after bottle of Vai's hair oil and a lurking fragrance around the house. The interest soon spread to pants. At first it was confined to an old pair of blue jeans which was all right since Vai had no time for the plantation. But the day soon arrived when Vai was late to work because all his pants had gone to school.

I thereupon limited pants-wearing to parties. This worked out fairly well because Vai had seven pairs of pants in various stages of disintegration. By spending the evening at home in his lavalava he could enable all his brothers to meet the latest social requirements.

But the shoe situation was serious. Bare feet look fine with lavalavas, but with pants at a party the boys felt undressed. Unfortunately Vai had only five specimens of footwear. Tala got his pumps, Losi got his everyday shoes, Pisa took the slippers, Pati settled for rubbers, and Falevalu located a pair of high-button patents left with Grandma by some ancient mariner. But Pita and Tapu had only one pair of cleated golf shoes between them. I suggested they wear one apiece, but they compromised by each attending half of the dance.

Their transition to Western ways proceeded most rapidly with regard to the plantation, however. Or was it that I just was not cut out to be a matai like my mother- and grandmother-in-law? For the first week the bright packages of vegetable seed attracted us all. As soon as school was over we scrambled up an 89-degree mountainside, felled trees, cleared bush, and uncovered an erodable strip of volcano which we lovingly called "the airport." Only Falevalu proved to have a green thumb. He thoughtfully covered the tomato sprouts with banana leaves against the burning sun. And tomatoes were about all that came up.

After a fortnight, however, our sons just failed to find their way to the mountaintop and we failed to find them until suppertime. Upon objecting I was informed that modern young men receive wages for their labor. I thought that over. Perhaps I could dole out movie money in the form of a small hourly wage. This might not only provide an incentive but introduce our sons to the world of business and balanced budgets. In a collective bargaining session we settled on ten cents an hour. Tomatoes and taros began to flourish and we planted ten new banana trees each day.

I had overlooked only one factor. For all my efforts I still was not a matai. Their real matai was sitting at home. As soon as the first taro roots began to swell, Grandma, Iakopo, Iosua, visiting parties, the pastor, and parents all made their customary claim to the labors of their young men. They harvested our plantation so efficiently that I was reduced to buying taro and bananas in the market place for our household.

Fortunately, however, matai do not like tomatoes. The boys picked this crop and sold it to stateside residents at prices which indicated a promising future in the business world. They pocketed the proceeds. After all, they had raised the tomatoes. I had an uneasy feeling that there was something uneconomic about paying people to raise their own food which they then sold at a profit while I fed them. But Vai assured me that it was just because I didn't understand the Samoan way of life.

I did begin to appreciate the Samoan word *musu*, however. It is a word meaning "I don't feel like working," and is entirely respectable. I began to feel decidedly musu myself, and decided to hold onto the plantation only until Iosua graduated from agriculture school. I had great hopes for Iosua. He had four years of agricultural training and was valedictorian of his class. A farmer was just what we needed. We gave a party for his graduation, complete down to the last pig. I formally presented him with the plantation. To my great distress he politely declined. He had just felt a "call" to the Methodist ministry which would entail seven years of study at Piula Seminary, starting immediately. The whole family glowed with pride at the prospect of another pastor in the family.

So I abandoned the plantation. These relatives had lived quite happily before I came and I might as well discover how they did it.

A month later the family hit economic bottom. They came to the house one day with empty baskets. There was nothing to eat and the grandchildren were crying. I informed them, quite truthfully, that there was also nothing in the till. Then I anxiously awaited the moment of revelation. They took my announcement with a nod of sympathy and trudged on to Aunt Mele who gave them a bunch of bananas. After dark they helped themselves to the mayor's breadfruit trees. Life continued as usual.

As the minds of our Samoan sons began to expand with high school knowledge, their little island seemed to shrink in proportion until it scarcely seemed worth living upon. For several years their restlessness was severely limited by our exchequer, but one day a navy recruiting team arrived in town. I delivered myself of some motherly sentiments about completing one's education, but it was like talking to a tropical breeze. Our boys, together with practically every other able-bodied male on the island, were in constant attendance at the recruiting station. My kitchen was referred to as a "galley." My meals became a "mess." I was introduced to stories which only a sailor should hear. But the Navy had some heartless restrictions about recruits. One concerned health. Falevalu, who had seen no exercise since the demise of the "airport," did fifty push-ups a day while reading a book entitled *Atlas—the Muscle Man*. Candidates were supposed to be American nationals, which eliminated Pati, who had been born in New Zealand Samoa. Candidates were also expected to pass an examination in English. This eliminated everyone but Falevalu.

Actually, however, these restrictions barred no Samoan with a spark of originality. Pati provided an eyewitness to his birth eighteen years before who took an oath regarding his American Samoan ancestry. Falevalu sat for the English exam three times, each time under a different name. He failed the first time under his own name, but passed the next two times as Tala and Pisa. Thanks to his linguistic ability two of our sons could see the world. But which two? The family selected Falevalu because, after all, he had actually passed the examination. Pisa was eliminated because it was so obvious that he didn't speak English. Losi had inadvertently married our housegirl, which disqualified him. That left Tapu, who proudly entered the Navy under the name Seaman Tala Ala'i.

Towards the end I must confess that I was almost as confused as the Navy as to the names and identities of my seven sons. I hardly dared address them in public for fear of ruining their navy careers. But we must have made a good selection. Both Falevalu and Tapu survived basic training and specialized in electronics. One would scarcely believe they had been born in a fale.

Lafi, who was still acting as Samoan matai of Washington, D.C., finally managed to send for Pati, Tala, and Pita. Losi's wife eventually earned enough to pay his way to Honolulu. Our sons left us almost as suddenly as they had arrived.

But I felt almost as well acquainted as Margaret Mead with the problems of Samoan adolescents.

CHAPTER FIVE

Co-op Encounter

Several of my sisters-in-law and I were on our second round of babies when I suddenly had an inspiration for pregnant wives. One day as I was unpacking gifts from my island relatives, a delicate little round mat caught my eye. I held it up to the light. It was so lovely it looked like lace. It had been created by women's fingers deftly winding pandanus-leaf strips around a stiff coconut midrib curled in a spiral. The stitches holding the spiral made a delicate design. What an ideal thing for a table mat! It would look lovely under a vase on a modern suburban coffee table.

The possibility that my sisters-in-law could produce something besides babies intrigued me. Next week I invited them over to a tea. It was well attended by portly ladies; not only my sisters-in-law but the pastor's wife, the matai's wife, and the aunt of the mayor were there. They sat in beaming silence in the more spacious chairs around the porch and we concentrated silently on tea and cakes for awhile. Then I passed around the mat that had inspired this meeting. Did they know how to make these? Would they like to sell some in America?

The proposition caused a torrent of excited chatter. Of

course they would like to sell mats. From what I could gather they were already talking about what they would do with the proceeds.

I steered them back to the problem of production, proposing that each submit a sample of her work. I would forward the best of these to a friend of mine who had a craft shop to see if they would sell. If we did get an order we would need an organization to see that good mats were produced in time for the boats.

That was the birth of the Fagatogo Craft Co-op. I suggested an election of officers but the idea caused confusion. They assumed that the high chief's wife should pass on the mats as her traditional role as leader of the village women demanded. There was some feeling that she might also appropriate the returns, so I reserved for myself the job of payment if it ever came to that.

Within a week the samples were in and I had a few problems on hand. What should be charged for such things in the States? I discovered the mats were not at all quick or easy to make. It took each lady a full day to weave a six-inch mat, and the larger sizes in proportion, to say nothing of the days involved finding, drying, and stripping pandanus leaves and coconut midribs for material. They agreed on fifty cents as a fair return for a six-inch mat.

Who was to pay for sending the samples and original order if we got one? There was only one possible answer to that. Me.

Our first order was from a small curio shop in Florida: twenty-seven dollars' worth. The ladies were beside themselves with joy when it came in. As the mats were submitted, I discovered more problems. Standardization was one headache. The order called for a set of eight dinner mats. The mayor's aunt produced eight lovely mats, but they didn't look even related. They were different sizes, different designs, different thicknesses, different colors. It bored her to make so many alike.

We also had a problem with quality. I held up a particularly disreputable piece to my sister-in-law. It looked like something I might have made myself.

"I thought you were the one who made that beautiful mat I first got as a gift," I said.

"I did," she replied. "But of course I save all my good mats for gifts."

My Western values slipped a cog, but I couldn't allow myself to get confused if our project was to succeed.

We also had the problem of deadlines. The shop naturally wanted its mats before the tourist season. There was only one boat from Pago that could make it. With sinking heart I met the pastor's wife setting off for a church dedication that involved a week's visit before she had finished her dozen. But if I was troubled, she was not. It was perfectly clear to her that religion took precedence over economics.

The worst problem of all was payment. I suppose that the curio shop was quite reasonable in wanting to see the mats before paying for them. But it was very unsatisfactory from our point of view. Transportation and return might take six months. The pastor's wife wanted her money for the church dedication even before she wove the mats. Everyone certainly expected to be paid when she handed in the work. I tried to explain the situation, but I could see the ladies were suspicious of me. As it turned out, I might as well have paid them outright from my pocket and saved the explanation. Long before payment finally arrived they had borrowed it from me anyway.

Despite its problems, the craft co-op did fairly well and continued to get small orders. Before long, a delegation of matai came to visit us from the five Tapuaiga villages beyond the end of the road on the south coast. Their talking chief was a most picturesque old gentleman. His thick hair was plastered with white lime; his wrinkled face bore a long black smear. He wore only a tapa held round the waist by an enormous leather belt.

With infinite dignity he seated himself on the floor and swung his switch of braided sennit fiber over his shoulder. The other chiefs seated themselves at the foot of my chairs in lieu of posts. After long words of thankfulness and the presentation of six kava sticks, they let us know that the Tapuaiga villages wanted to make square pandanus table mats to sell in the States. This was no small proposition since the villages could muster several hundred weavers, and, according to their talking chief, could produce thousands of dozens with machinelike regularity and uniformity. Some form of production they said, was absolutely essential to Tapuaiga. The matai had been unable to pay their five-dollar annual head tax to the government and they were, according to the chief, in imminent danger of being locked up as a body.

I laid the matter before Vai. In view of the village crisis Vai felt we should accept the proposition. But after my experience with the Fagatogo co-op I insisted on some conditions. There must be bylaws, a production manager to assign and inspect work, a business manager to handle payments, and a board of directors to investigate anything that might seem suspicious. Each weaver must submit ten cents with his first sample to cover mailing, and the co-op must keep 10 per cent of all returns as a reserve to cover rejects, losses, and future freight charges. Each weaver should receive his pay individually. I congratulated myself on my foresight.

The delegation thanked us profusely and returned to inform the village weavers. Several weeks later we were invited to Tapuaiga to establish the organization.

It was a beautiful day. Great white breakers were booming in on pinnacles of black rock at each end of Amanave Beach and the fales were clustered around a little white sand cove in between.

We were ushered into a house decorated from ceiling to floor with lacings of leaves and flowers. The matai from the other four villages had come in over the mountains the night before and we shook hands all around. The village maiden, who squeezed the kava in the traditional ceremony of welcome, was stunning, and since I came in the capacity of business advisor rather than merely as Vai's wife I was honored with the first cup. The photogenic talking chief looked even better in a fale than on my front porch. He argued at length with another chief as to who should have the privilege of welcoming us, but the outcome of this ceremonial debate was never really in doubt. After a long half hour his opponent gracefully conceded. When we finally got to the welcome speech itself it lasted well into the afternoon.

After the speeches came the feast: pigs, lobsters, turtle, octopus, chop suey, palusami, potato salad, taro, bananas, rice, and raspberry Kool-Aid—enough to fill all sixty chiefs and also baskets for their relatives. I couldn't help but feel that the cash value of the same feast would have given them quite a start on that five-dollar head tax they needed. But mine was a Western viewpoint.

Late in the evening we finally got around to organizing the co-operative. In deference to me they approved my by-laws, but it was simply a friendly gesture. There was no need to elect a production manager. Who could organize and police the production of each family better than the matai themselves? So we had about thirty production managers. And why elect a co-op board? The village council, composed of the same matai was the natural institution for the job, especially since it had thought of the idea in the first place. Paying the weavers individually was out of the question. The matai had to pay the original ten cent investment since in each family the matai always held the family funds. The government held him responsible for the head tax. The family depended on him for support. So it was only logical that any payments should also go to him. The only procedure that actually followed my bylaws was the business manager position for whom there was no traditional Samoan counterpart.

I was always glad I didn't insist on adherence to the bylaws. The matai proved quite capable of getting their families to produce good mats and on time. They were in a position to cancel visiting trips just before shipments, which no one else could have done. And the village council outdid itself in policing co-op accounts. The poor business agent had to spend days on the mat trying to explain to the chiefs why the producers didn't get exactly what the purchaser in the States paid. They didn't believe him. To save the business agent from being run out of the village I made an emergency trip to Amanave with full details about packing costs, insurance, freight, and duty.

The village council never did feel happy about the 10 per cent reserve. The business agent taught them how to calculate it but he couldn't convince them that the bank was a safe place to keep it. He couldn't explain the bank statement because he didn't understand it. I went out on another rescue mission only to find that I couldn't explain it either. The reserve had vanished. The business agent resigned and it took me two weeks to discover that the bank statement was correct. There was nothing in the reserve because the chiefs themselves had already borrowed it for a celebration.

But Tapuaiga did produce. The first order from a department store in Detroit netted fifty-two dollars. I sent a letter to Amanave when the check arrived. Next morning two singing busloads pulled up before our house. Out poured a good proportion of the population of Tapuaiga. Someone sent for a barrel of beef and a case of biscuits. A feast of rejoicing was soon in progress. Tapuaiga stayed in town for two days. When time came to present them with the fifty-two dollars, they were also presented with bus and grocery bills amounting to considerably more.

We sat in a circle on the floor of my porch to discuss this situation. The talking chief insisted that the food bills be forwarded to the department store in Detroit. After all, wasn't it their order that had caused the rejoicing? The rest of the village council readily agreed. I dissented, and it was the first and only occasion upon which I ever won a debate with a talking chief.

It is probably fortunate that we did not forward the bills to Detroit since that particular contact led to a two-thousand-dollar order from an import firm in New York. The island buzzed with the news. Five other villages begged to start co-ops.

Tapuaiga produced the mats, hundreds of dozens. It took several buses to bring them into town. It was at this juncture that I made a fatal mistake. I remembered the huge box that had brought our household furniture to American Samoa. If we could pack the mats into something like that we could save hundreds of small parcels that might get lost on the way. I asked the Tapuaiga carpenters to build a box of this kind. They obligingly made one the size of a room. To avoid bursting at the seams it was braced with logs of solid hardwood, fresh from the mountains. The freight clerk wanted to know how much it weighed. That was an idle question since it couldn't be put on the scales. No one could move it.

Eventually we unpacked it and pulled the empty box out on the wharf with a truck. We refilled it where the ship's crane could swing it aboard. I was greatly relieved to see it start off down the harbor.

The import firm in New York was not at all happy to see it arrive, however. I got an irate cable from them describing their problems in getting it off the dock and into their warehouse. Did I think the port of New York could handle *anything?*

We never got a further order from that firm but we did get others. Tapuaiga had its feasts, the government got its head tax, and we all learned something about business.

As soon as the craft co-ops began to earn money, Vai decided that they needed a retail co-op to spend it in. Organizing a co-operative store was not difficult at all. He simply called a meeting in the high school auditorium and all his friends showed up. Bylaws and elections took half an hour and that was all there was to it for everyone—except myself. I had been elected manager.

It was not hard to get members. Everyone seemed anxious to join. My only problem was to find a store. Poking around one day, I made a discovery. In a dusty, unused warehouse I uncovered the remains of a navy commissary, unused since the military left. It was a dream of a little self-service market with white enameled shelves; two walk-in refrigerators; dairy, vegetable, and meat display cases; electric saws; scales; and even push-baskets. I rushed down to the administration building to ask for an option on it. Apparently the acting governor didn't know about it either, but, once it had been discovered, word got around fast enough. The merchants put up quite a clamor when they heard what the co-op was after. That little commissary disappeared overnight. Medical Supply took the shelves and refrigerators. The hospital took the meat grinders. The largest store in town rented the display cases. The co-op got one broken cash register.

Together with the cash register I finally settled down in a little shack that had formerly housed military band instruments. It wasn't an ideal location commercially, but it was right between our house and the police station.

Stocking the store was another problem. Our $2,500 of share capital didn't go very far, because stateside boats arrived four to six months apart and we had to supply ourselves for the duration. I decided it would be sensible to major in sugar and sardines.

The laws of American Samoa did not provide for cooperatives. Such forms of enterprise apparently were not legally possible. After several weeks of consultation with the Attorney General it was decided the only legal solution was a partnership with ninety-three members. I had a disturbing feeling that if ninety-two members resigned I might be left alone with the invoices, but it was too late now.

First month's sales amounted to about $1,200 and net profit to a little over $90. Shortly thereafter we ran out of both sugar and sardines and closed down to await the next boat.

The co-op did work, however. At the end of the first year we found we could declare a 3 per cent patronage rebate. From an economic point of view this should certainly have been reinvested in sardines, but from a Samoan point of view what we needed was a gala distribution of checks and a feast.

For the occasion we rented the YWCA and asked the governor to address us. He refused, and we settled on a movie called *The Rochdale Story* which we borrowed from the South Pacific Commission.

The major attraction, of course, was food. I banned borrowing from the co-op shelves since I was tired of sardines, and the occasion was provided for Samoan style. Every matai member was asked to bring a pig; every matai's wife a salad and a cake; everyone else four bundles of fish and five palusami plus ten baked taro. Our one industrial member was to provide orangeade from his homemade bottling works. Stateside members were responsible for ice cream.

Everything was forthcoming except the ice cream. The display of food was staggering. So that everyone could fully appreciate the effect I inadvisably suggested that we arrange the food buffet style. I had completely forgotten that Samoans think of feasting not in terms of plates, but of baskets. When I saw the first little old lady in the line select a cake and pop it whole into her basket, I smiled tolerantly. But as the line proceeded I was in tears. Young men were lowering whole cases of orangeade out of the window to their friends below. The chief of police retired with a whole roast pig on his shoulder. Everything was in an uproar. Statesiders at the end of the line got nothing at all. I trudged home hungry myself. What a terrible debacle!

Next morning the co-op feast was the talk of the town. From every side I heard of our success. It seems we had outdone the paramount chiefs in lavish generosity. The chiefs customarily seated their guests on the ground and then allowed anything within arm's reach. But the co-op had allowed a procession and the full sweep of the table! Our membership doubled.

From then on the co-op expanded rapidly, aided by an economic boom on the island. The fish cannery across the bay which had been closed for six years for lack of fish suddenly reopened its doors. A Japanese fishing smack had discovered that monster tuna roamed the sea a few thousand feet below where American fishermen had angled in vain. They caught a nine-hundred-pound giant just outside the harbor.

The arrival of the Japanese fishing fleet caused some distress among local merchants whose shelves were loaded with cans of salmon from Alaska, and sardines from South Africa. The government tried in vain to get them to handle

fresh fish. The island refrigerator plant overflowed and the governor got desperate.

As usual, the co-op was out of sardines and waiting for the next boat. We informed the governor that we would be glad to market his fish if he would provide us with a store, a refrigerator, an electric meat cutter, display cases, and a good cash register. He did, and most of the commissary miraculously reappeared.

We fixed up a large screened room at the corner of the refrigerator plant. I was proud of it. It looked like a distant cousin to a supermarket when the gleaming display cases were installed. Fish sales were enormous for the first few days until the Samoans had time to make friends with the little Japanese fishermen. Thereafter most of us got our fish free and there was only a moderate call for it at the market. I say "us" because the sons who were still with us soon had Japanese friends who kept us well supplied at home, too.

I was quite satisfied with having reacquired the navy commissary so unexpectedly, but my satisfaction was short lived. It was one thing to manage a little shack near our house, and quite another to handle a "supermarket" at the other end of town in addition. I had to hire managers and clerks to help.

We had plenty of applications for these new jobs. Many volunteered to work for nothing. But I had learned about "free" labor from Lua and declined. Apparently, however, I hadn't learned enough.

At the end of the first month my books showed a hundred-dollar deficit at the small store. Since my bookkeeping is not always to be relied upon, I let it go. Next month the deficit was up towards two hundred dollars and I notified the co-op board. They couldn't locate the problem either until one matai heard that the chief clerk was building a new fale. Then he found the leak immediately. The clerk's carpenter was appearing at the co-op every day to collect his rations and he had many relatives. It was all quite within the traditions of the *fa'aSamoa*.

We fired the clerk and the carpenter, but to my consternation, next month's books showed a deficit at both stores. None of the new staff was building a fale, but eventually we singled out the assistant bookkeeper. In the process of banking the daily cash he had modified the deposit slips and turned over the balance to his matai. The Attorney General and I wanted to make him a good public example, but the co-op board refused.

"If you do that," said Vai, "the boy will go to jail, the matai will be angry, and we will never get our money back. Handle it my way and we'll come out all right."

We handled it his way. He went out to visit the boy's matai. In a long, polite, and friendly conversation he pointed out that the co-op belonged to many matai. They would not look with favor at a matai who helped himself. The father promptly repaid the co-op.

Next month things were worse than ever at the fish market. From the stock cards I could see that we were losing three-pound cans of corned beef by the case. But how? Day after day I policed the store and saw nothing irregular. Night after night board members stood guard, but no one broke in. Three-pound cans of meat continued to disappear, however, and we were completely mystified.

One night a board member was checking the locks. He came round to the heavy refrigerator door separating our store from the central corridor of the ice plant. We never used this door and the huge rusty padlock was invincible. But his eye fell upon the hinge pins on the other side of the door. They were strangely shiny. He pushed them and they rose out of their fittings as if they had been greased. The door fell open easily from the wrong side. He tested the other doors down the corridor. They did the same. Evidently someone had been availing himself of the supplies of the co-op, the government, and all the other stores in town.

The co-op got unwanted fame from the discovery. Other merchants spread the word that the co-op had inventory losses. In vain we countered that they had been losing too; our books were open and theirs were not. Some of our biggest shareholders withdrew and we were left with fewer sardines than ever. We closed the smaller store.

The third year we were fortunate enough to find three Samoans who had retired from the navy band. In the course of their careers they had had some experience with commissaries. We turned the co-op management over to them. They never quite understood Rochdale principles and the store began to look more like a three-man partnership than a co-operative, but they gave me a good opportunity to retire. It was high time. A third little Ala'i was in the offing and Samoan business is no occupation for a mother. It is apt to take twenty-four hours off one's day and ten years off one's life.

Despite my business experience I still had much to learn about Samoan economics. One of the most commonly used words in the Samoan language is *fa'amolemole* which I soon learned means "please" in the imperative sense. One day I received my first letter in Samoan. I tore it open eagerly and found it was from my mother-in-law. After the customary references to the Trinity she wrote,

"*Fa'amolemole lava ua faa'lavelavea a'u.*"

I rushed to Vai.

"What is a *fa'alavelave?*" I asked. "Your mother's got one."

Vai looked up in surprise.

"Have you been in Samoa this long without discovering what a *fa'alavelave* is?"

I nodded.

"Well, it means trouble, any kind of trouble—like a wedding, a christening, a church dedication, or something like that," he explained.

"Sounds more like fun than trouble," I said.

"That's because you haven't read the rest of the letter," Vai replied. "My mother's trouble is that a daughter of her second cousin is getting married. She wants you to supply the wedding cake, a wedding dress, and your sewing machine as a wedding present."

"Now I understand your definition," I said sourly. "And you write your mother that a wedding cake wouldn't stand the boat trip to Upolu; that I haven't the vaguest idea of the size of her second cousin's daughter; and that if I gave her my sewing machine I couldn't make lavalavas for her sons and grandsons."

"Listen," said Vai patiently, "apparently you still don't understand the *fa'aSamoa.* You simply cannot refuse to help a relative who has a fa'alavelave. How do you think all that food for our wedding feast was collected? Don't worry about the size of the wedding dress, she will be getting three or four others and probably won't want to wear yours anyway."

Despite the way I had once benefited, I took a thorough dislike to fa'alavelaves. It seemed that the slightest occasion of the most distant relative required a case of sardines or a barrel of beef. Even the most joyous occasion was well named a "trouble" from my point of view. And every "please" was apparently an inescapable demand. I lived in constant fear that someone in the family would marry or graduate or have a baby.

In my distress I soon discovered that I was not the only one suffering from this custom. Everyone I knew had debts in the stores, compounded with each successive fa'alavelave.

As assistant personnel officer, Vai was aware of it too.

"These government employees," he said one day, "have a

terrible time meeting their fa'alavelaves. What they need is a credit union, like the ones in the States, where they can borrow when they are in trouble."

In my misery, I sympathized with any solution.

So Vai called a meeting to discuss credit unions. The response was enthusiastic. Each credit-union member agreed to have five dollars deducted from his wages each month as a compulsory credit-union share. Loans were to be given at 1 per cent interest per month. How could we lose on bylaws as conservative as that?

When it came to deciding what type of situation we would give loans for, I had a qualm.

"Let's restrict loans to productive projects only," I suggested to the meeting.

A series of negative speakers immediately responded. What good would a credit union be if it couldn't be used for fa'alavelaves? They were the very thing Samoans wanted money *for*. Vai gallantly put my proposition to a vote. Since credit unions are democratic organizations, I retired as a dissatisfied minority of one.

Within three months credit-union deposits soared to over two thousand dollars a month. Weddings were better than ever. Two more credit unions wanted to organize. Vai estimated the credit union could pay 3 per cent interest on shares by the end of the year.

But there were problems too. So much money was involved that the Attorney General required that the treasurer of the credit union—Vai, of course—be bonded. That was a wise precaution but no United States company would bond him. The Attorney General impounded all our personal savings (such as they were) as security on the venture.

A second problem was that bookkeeping mounted with membership and shares. Soon Vai was spending all night on the books and any minutes he could spare at the office.

His boss frowned upon the credit union even though it was for government employees.

A surprising new reason for loans developed. When I asked two brothers why they had borrowed fifty dollars they replied that they had no immediate use for it but that it was smart business to take loans. The more loans, the more interest, and therefore the greater the rebate the credit union could give them on their shares. I spent an uneasy night trying to figure out what was wrong with that theory. The credit union was obviously getting beyond me.

For a year the Government Employees Credit Union prospered. Every month its entire capital was loaned by the end of the first week, and recouped by the last when the government deduction check came in. The governor's cook borrowed two thousand dollars at a special long-term, low-interest rate to build himself a house. The co-op store borrowed to stock sardines. There were only two bad debts.

Suddenly, one month, the government did not send the credit union its customary wage-deduction check. Vai rushed to the Attorney General, and was informed that the governor had declared it illegal to garnishee wages. The rule was directed at the stores, but the credit union would have to abide by it too.

Vai stopped all further loans, but it was too late. The money was already out. News of the governor's decision spread rapidly among the members. Vai hopefully called for a continuation of monthly share savings with each member bringing his own deposit to the office. Only two sweet little nurses responded.

Our personal savings were forthwith impounded, but even that left a sizeable gap between shares owed and cash available. At least two thirds of the members refused to repay what they had borrowed, buttressed by a law that no Samoan can be sued for a debt of more than twenty-five dollars. Great, sudden, and complete was the fall of the credit union.

Pleading with members was futile. When, soberer and wiser, we left Tutuila we turned over two thousand dollars of outstanding debts to the bank for collection. The bank was in a position to bring more pressure than the credit union. Five years later the bank finally succeeded in repaying all outstanding shares.

I avenged myself by writing an article for the South Pacific Commission dedicated to experts who believe that cooperative enterprise is the key to the economic advancement of South Pacific islands. It was never printed.

CHAPTER SIX

Salani and Its Past

Eighty miles from Tutuila, across the heaving Pacific, are the islands of Western Samoa. Slowly but hopefully these islands were in the process of working their way from New Zealand trusteeship towards independence. The 1954 Constitutional Convention of Western Samoa fascinated Vai with the future that it had opened up.

"There's life in that legislature over there," he told me. "When a chief gets up to talk everyone listens whether they like him or not, because the game is a real one. Here the chiefs can't really call the tune because Uncle Sam always has to pay the piper. Someday the Samoans in Upolu will be running a country while the Samoans here in Tutuila will be dancing for tourists."

I could just see where this sort of talk was leading us. Some recessive gene left in me by a Revolutionary ancestor responded to Vai's enthusiasm for independence. Certainly there must be some place by now in Western Samoa for a Samoan with a master's degree in public administration. Trained Samoans would be needed in this great experiment.

We made a week's trip to Apia to talk with the director of government employment, a fatherly New Zealander who had apparently acquired his own views of self-government.

"My boy," he said to Vai, with a kindly clap on the shoulder, "let me give you a piece of advice. If you come to work for us you would only get half of what you make in Tutuila which is only half again of what you would make in the States. For a person with your education there is really no future in a place like this. You wouldn't be happy here. The best thing you can do is to return to the States."

That did it. Vai determined to go to Western Samoa, employed or not. No Samoan was ever kept off his own islands by the insignificant problem of earning a living. Not with breadfruit and coconuts dropping from every tree.

"Do you remember my thesis on Salani?" Vai asked.

"I should," I replied, "I was intimately connected with it."

"Well, next August the first road will be opened up across the mountains to the southeast coast of Upolu. It will come within a few miles of Salani, very close to my family land in Falealili District. Now is the time to start our plantation. We will carry out all those ideas we had about developing Salani."

My mind shot back to the thesis; water supplies, hydropower, a co-operative marketing association, a set of laws for the village *fono*. Three years, three craft co-ops, two stores, and a defunct credit union ago, these ideas sounded simpler than they did now. I had a disturbing feeling that with my present experience I couldn't write an acceptable thesis at all. It would have to be of such modest proportions.

But Vai was made of sterner stuff. Before returning to Tutuila we decided to visit Salani to see how it would respond to the proposition of progress. Besides, I was curious to see the place we had described with such loving detail in the thesis. We stopped in at the Lands Survey Office in Apia to determine the most feasible route over the mountains.

"Oh, it's easy these days," the surveyor said opening a

map. "The road is open as far as the top of the Mafa Pass here in the central range. From there you can take the trail down the mountains to Lotofaga and Salani on foot."

We measured the track on his map. Four inches should equal four miles. I could make that all right. We thanked him and hired a taxi to the Mafa Pass.

A tourist folder describes the road east along the north shore of Upolu as "the most scenic in the South Pacific." It does not exaggerate. Clean-swept fales nestle in each little cove, and the foaming white Pacific crashes against the black rocks on every cape. It was Saturday when we passed, and everywhere the men were fishing, tossing round nets into the surf or bobbing around in little outrigger canoes. Women and children waded along the reef looking for shell-fish.

At Falefa the road turned sharply inland through a wide, lush valley filled with coconut, cocoa, and banana trees all growing in happy confusion. Above us sharp volcanic peaks rose 3,000 feet from the sea.

At Falevao the taxi started up the steep central range, four miles of incredible hairpin turns, alternating views of sheer mountain waterfalls with vistas of the Pacific far below. It was breathtaking to the eye and also to the stomach. The road was hardly of American proportions. Barely twelve feet of flat dirt separated the cliff at our left from the abyss at our right. If we had met a car coming down we would probably have had to back all the way down the mountain before we could pass each other.

At the top we stopped to recover our composure and cool the car. A lazy little cloud drifted through the mountain gap just above our heads and we looked off into the sharp, uninhabited jumble of the central range. In the valley far below wisps of smoke from village outdoor ovens curled up through the coconut trees. It was truly a country for the gods.

A mile further on the road came to a muddy end in the

midst of a dense rain forest. Great vines slithered up the
many-trunked banyan trees and giant ferns spread delicately
over our heads. It was quiet, timeless, and elemental as
only the deep forest can be. When the taxi turned and left
us we suddenly felt very small and lonely in this vast
panorama of God's splendor. We tried to hurry down the
trail but couldn't. We sank half way to our knees in thick
red mud. One sticky mile later I sat down to rest.

"This is hard work," I commented. "I'm thirsty."

"We should be close to the Fagatoloa River," Vai said.
"I'll go for a drink." He disappeared.

I wondered idly how he would transport a drink in his
bare hands. Twenty minutes later he returned with ice cold
water wrapped up in a big leaf. If one must walk in the
virgin forest without equipment, it is obviously wise to
travel with a Samoan. No one else can carry water in a leaf.

After another mile I sat down again.

"Now I'm hungry," I said, waiting to see what would happen. Vai turned to examine a split tree trunk nearby. In a
few moments he pulled an enormous, green, accordion-
pleated worm out of a hole and offered it to me.

"Ugh," I said. He popped it into his own mouth with a
look of utter delight. The thought of it cured my appetite
for the rest of the day.

The sun rose to its zenith without a perceptible change
in the cool semidarkness through which we were walking.
It occurred to me that we certainly must have covered four
miles by now. In the middle of the afternoon quite unexpectedly the forest opened onto an enormous gorge. The
bank plunged down four hundred feet vertically from our
toes and the opposite bank rose as sharply a quarter of a
mile away. The chasm appeared so suddenly that I almost
walked into it. Sweeping my eye up the foaming river at
the bottom I caught my breath. At the upper end a graceful cataract leaped out of a narrow crack and plunged two

hundred feet into a mist of foam and rainbows. I couldn't take my eyes from it for fear it would vanish as suddenly as it had appeared.

"Sopoaga Falls," Vai murmured. "What a place to live!"

Soon after that we came to a fork in the trail. Our map showed nothing so we were perplexed. We tried one, then the other, and had to admit we were lost.

Suddenly a lithe brown figure arose from the bushes right beside us. I was startled. This man must have been watching us all along, but he blended so well with the leaves that we never saw him. He chatted amiably with Vai for some minutes then pointed to the right fork.

"I never heard of walking all day to go four miles," I said. "Ask him how much further this place is."

We could elicit nothing more definite than a cheerful, "Not far"—but I could imagine that ten miles was "not far" to a physique like his.

At the end of the afternoon the forest finally gave way to coconut plantations and before long we heard the roaring of the Pacific surf. We turned west up the coast through several tiny thatched villages bustling with the evening meal. It was already dark when we finally emerged on a sand spit. A wide river swirled here out of the dark forest and into the sea.

"There is Salani," Vai said reverently, pointing to the further shore. "I haven't seen it since I was a boy. Look, our old fale has gone from the point. Otherwise it is just the same."

I strained my eyes eagerly. Tiny lights twinkled out of the fales and danced upon the river.

"How do we get over there?" I asked feeling as if I were almost home.

"Swim," said Vai. "Follow me."

We bundled our clothes and holding them high above our heads paddled across the gloomy river. On the other

side three women came down to draw water. Seeing two
strangers emerge from the river seemed to cause them no
surprise. They nodded pleasantly. But when Vai introduced
himself there was a buzz of excitement. Little boys ran
around with the word. People poked their heads out of fales
as we walked across the village square amid a gathering
crowd to a round fale perched high on a pile of stones.
Women were already pulling down rolls of mats from the
rafters for our convenience. I met one of Vai's brothers and
his wife. In no time we were seated in a circle of welcome.
Chiefs, baskets of taro, and bundles of fish began to arrive
as if we had been expected all along. With them came the
village pastor in a stiff white coat and white lavalava. The
hollow log drummed the familiar signal for family worship,
and people disappeared dutifully into their houses. Soon,
like the rest of the village, we were intoning the evening
prayer. A dozen different hymns drifted over to us across
the village square. We were already a part of village life.
After prayers the women set leaf trays before us and we
topped off the taro and fish with a cup of rich, dark, hand-
pounded cocoa with globules of cocoa butter floating on
the top and particles of bean in the bottom.

The food, the dim light, the exercise of the day and the
hum of voices made me feel utterly relaxed. I leaned back
and squinted drowsily up at the roof bindings, out to the
reef, and back to the circle of eager faces. It occurred to
me that this could easily have been an evening discussion
350 years ago—even the names of the chiefs were the same.
I looked at them and thought of Salani's past.

Back in 1600, I recalled from Vai's thesis, the predeces-
sors of these very chiefs were suffering a burning humiliation. They had no high titles, as did leaders in other
districts. At the great island gatherings no post of honor was
reserved for them; when kings were made or married they

got no share of the fine mats; when wars were to be waged they weren't even consulted. It was intolerable.

Finally two young men, one from Salani and the other from the neighboring village of Satalo, resolved to take action. From their plantations they pulled the most succulent young taro. They grated these and mixed them with coconut cream and cooked them carefully in leaf packages on the hot rocks of their ovens. Then they cut the sweet gelatinous mass into cubes known as *fa'aausi*, Samoa's closest approach to candy. With these as a gift they started across the mountains to visit Queen Salamasina who was living on the northwest coast of the island.

Salamasina was a lady worth visiting. Due to fortuitous circumstances of birth, and the political machinations of her influential talking chiefs, she was the first person in the history of Samoa to collect all four ruling titles in her own person. She was Samoa's first and most famous Queen. During the sixty years of her reign the island enjoyed a blessed respite from almost constant civil wars.

The Queen found the fa'aausi candy from Falealili delicious. As an expression of her gratitude she gave the two young men high talking-chief titles. One was henceforth known as Lalo of Satalo, and the other as Ofo of Salani. (I glanced at their descendants of the same name, sitting in the circle near me.)

The two young men returned home in triumph. Falealili now had status thanks to their efforts. But their joy soon palled. What, after all, was the use of being talking chiefs unless they had a high chief to talk for? Like capable talking chiefs everywhere, they plotted secretly to remedy this unfortunate situation and make Falealili a district to be reckoned with. At length they developed a daring plan.

Salamasina had just had a baby. In the child's veins ran the blood of the four great families of Upolu plus that of the powerful Tonumaipe'a clan of Savaii, soldiers of the famous war goddess Nafanua. To everyone's delight the baby was a boy. Seldom in history has one little child managed to consolidate so much dignity in one small frame.

Lalo and Ofo hastened back over the mountains to be present at the great feast in honor of the baby's umbilical cord. Every other prominent chief on the island did the same. The royal village was crowded with titled guests. Its fales were gaily laced with leaves and flowers, and its cookhouses groaned with food. In Salamasina's house the baby was passed around for inspection and compliments. Ofo asked to hold it. The laughter and excitement continued. Some time later Salamasina asked for her child. No one was just sure who had it. Probably someone had taken it to another house to sleep. It was not until evening that a general search was made. The baby could not be found.

The Queen was disconsolate, but under the circumstances little could be done. Since all the chiefs had gathered so much food, it would be unthinkably discourteous not to continue the feasting. After a few weeks of searching it became clear that the baby was not in any of the more prominent places on the island. Salamasina gave her son up for lost.

But on the south coast, the sparsely populated district of Falealili could not permanently conceal its joy. Ofo and Lalo had kidnaped a King! He was growing up healthy and happy in the village of Salani. A year or so later word got back to Salamasina and she herself set out over the mountains to reclaim her son.

A visit from the Queen! It was a great occasion for all of Falealili District, but especially for Salani. The situation inspired its noblest efforts. Ofo, Lalo, and everybody else outdid themselves in offering pigs, taro, fish, fa'aausi, and oratory. They told the Queen they had named the baby Tapu, after his father, and that their lives were worth living now they had a chief of unquestioned lineage as their own. They assured Salamasina he was being as well cared for as any mother could possibly wish.

Having someone to talk for apparently brought out the best in the talking chiefs, Lalo and Ofo. The Queen was greatly impressed with their oratory. She was also impressed with their generosity. In the end she said they could keep Tapu.

Salamasina must have been impressed with Salani as well, nestled as it was between the virgin forest, the Fagatoloa River and the sea. When she wearied of the pomp of office she retired there to live with her son. Any villager today can show you where she bathed and trapped pigeons. She is buried in the nearby village of Lotofaga.

Lalo and Ofo had done well. Tapu, with his ancestry, had no difficulty proliferating titles. He himself took the title Tele and founded the village of Sasatele across the river. His son, by his fortunate marriage, connected Salani with the famous Safenu title of Lefa. His grandson was the first Sifu. A great-grandson did his part for the title shortage by dividing his title, Fuima, among his seven sons. And a great-great-grandson did best of all. He was adopted by the highest chief of the eastern district and given the title Tupua. One of the two present Heads of State is a Tupua and Salani is one of the villages from which he derives his power. No one today could possibly accuse Salani of lack of titular dignity.

Lalos, Ofos, Teles, Sifus, and Fuimas, present and past, blurred together in my mind with the rumbling of the surf and the flickering of the lamp. Kidnaped babies came and went. I stretched my weary legs, rolled over on my mat, and felt time slip away completely. I was fast asleep.

CHAPTER SEVEN

Salani and Its Present

Next morning I awoke to find myself in the present. The school blackboard had been brought in during the night. It was covered with complicated pictures of wheels.

"What's that?" I asked Vai as he came back from a wash in the river.

"Oh," he laughed, "the chiefs are all for progress. That is a picture of the hydroelectric plant we are going to build on Sopoaga Falls."

I had an awful feeling from the picture that Vai didn't know any more about turbines and generators than I did.

"Don't you think we should start first by clearing a road and introducing the cart wheel?" I asked.

"No indeed," said Vai, "you must always start with what people want; and these chiefs want an electric plant."

My own wants were simpler at the moment. I whispered an anxious question to Vai. He shook his head and whispered to our host's wife. She nodded and whispered to an aunt. They consulted for a few moments. Yes, one of the pastors had such a thing. They beckoned me to follow them and we started out across the village square towards the ocean. In no time we were surrounded by a mob of children, laughing, giggling, and calling, *"Palagi."* At the other end of the village I caught sight of a small house set out over the water, reached by a single wobbly board. The crowd stopped on the shore and watched with interest while I teetered across. I shook the door, anxious to close it between me and all those eyes, but it was held fast by a rusty lock. I teetered back and demonstrated the lock problem in sign language. The children let out a whoop as they grasped my meaning. We proceeded back to the pastor's house which was filling with chiefs for a special meeting. The company was duly informed of my difficulty and everyone began to look high and low for the key. I was frightfully embarrassed.

"That's a strange thing to lose," I grumbled to Vai as he entered with an inquiring expression.

"Not so odd," he replied. "That little house probably hasn't been used since the last missionary was here."

The missionary must have taken the key with him. Anyway it could not be found. I paraded seaward again, this time accompanied by the pastor and chiefs as well as the children. Someone kindly broke the lock with a stone. When I teetered back to shore the waiting crowd gave a cheer. Thereafter I quietly used the facilities that God had provided for such villages, like everyone else.

The fono reassembled and I sat close behind Vai, trying to make my presence as inconspicuous as possible under the circumstances.

The village fono usually meets on Monday with the chiefs sitting according to rank at their appropriate posts. After kava, the mayor may introduce a few dull subjects such as the number of coconut beetles to be collected, or the fact that pigs should really be kept out of the houses. Nobody listens. The mayor's job was the idea of some foreigner who wanted to "improve" village life, as if such a thing were conceivable. It is perpetuated only by its ten-pound annual stipend. Some needy matai, usually a low one, can generally be found who will submit to the humiliation of boring his betters. And they, in their tolerance, will put up with it providing it does not interfere with the real business of chiefs. The real business of chiefs is dedications, visiting parties, or title disputes which affect family status or the dignity of the village. On such matters they spring into eager, sometimes even violent, action. Vai had told me of that dreadful night in his childhood when a former Ofo had eloped with the wife of a former Tele. Elopements between ordinary mortals can be forgiven but one which involves the dignity of a high chief rocks the foundations of society. The culprit was caught, woven into a coconut leaf basket, tied to a pole, and presented to the offended chief for roasting. Only the fact that a clever village pastor requested his share of the basket uncooked saved Ofo's life, but he was banished from Salani forever. The incident split the village in two. Over the years some chiefs landed in the hospital and others in jail, as this elopement came up for renewed discussion. It was twenty years before the chiefs met again as a single fono.

But now they were here as a single body, at a special meeting to discuss the hydroelectric plant.

Vai introduced the idea of a taro-marketing co-op as a means of paying for the electric plant. There was a polite silence. He tried again with the idea of a store. The meeting sprang to life. The school blackboard reappeared and somebody drew something distressingly like a department store. I could just see a branch of Macy's on the south shore of Upolu with chiefs running in and out of revolving doors. Apparently they could see it too.

Vai introduced the marketing co-op again as a way of paying for the department store. Silence again.

"Well, how *are* you going to pay for it?" he asked.

That was simple, someone replied. They would borrow

five hundred pounds and repay it by selling to each other on credit. Again I had the distressing feeling that there was something I didn't quite comprehend about Samoan economics. I began a speech to the effect that sometime, somewhere, production must equal consumption, but was met with incredulous stares.

"Stop trying to discourage them," whispered Vai menacingly. "Can't you see they don't like the idea?"

In the end we compromised. Instead of borrowing five hundred pounds, each matai was to buy five-pound shares in the store, finding the money where he could. Vai's brother was selected treasurer. We provided him with an old credit-union sharebook and purchased the first share to show how it was done.

"Does Salani claim the forest inland from its plantations?" Vai asked, thinking of our future home.

"Of course," the chiefs replied. "The land was once taken by the Germans but it was given back to us by New Zealand because our District remained loyal to the government during the Mau Rebellion."

"Do we have a written deed to prove it?" asked Vai. No one knew, so two chiefs agreed to accompany us to Apia next day to find out.

Vai explained our plan to start a plantation in the forest several miles behind the village and the chiefs kindly offered to help us clear it.

After the fono, Vai and I took a walk around the village. Salani, I discovered, was not as attractive as some Samoan villages. Its 325 inhabitants lived in fales of rather ancient vintage. These were surrounded not with white sand and coconuts, but with black lava rock and breadfruit. The ruins of a church formed the center of one end of the village, and a Methodist church, soon to join its predecessor, graced the other. The beaches were covered with driftwood and weeds, and a large boat had sunk in the mouth of the

river. The school was a dilapidated little fale at the back,
but its occupants were lively enough. They rose as a body
to sing me their only English song, the title of which was
"Look Both Ways Before You Cross the Street." They sang
it with such conviction that I could scarcely believe that
they were eight miles from the nearest road and hardly in
imminent danger of traffic accidents.

But though their genius was certainly not economic,
one could scarcely call Salani villagers lazy. They seemed
to be involved in a great number of organizational activities. Every chief's wife, for example, held the rank of her
husband in a very dignified organization known as the
Faletua ma Tausi. This organization conducted "visitations." On "visitation" day members made the rounds of
each other's homes to count sheets, pillow cases, mats, and
mosquito nets. Woe to the wife who could not produce the
proper number. She paid a heavy fine. Apparently this was
looked at more as a game than as an inspiration to good
housekeeping, for my sister-in-law promptly arranged to
borrow my sheets for the next "visitation" day. Other ladies
had special chests in which to lock these precious items
lest they become used and worn.

The young men had an organization of their own known
as the *aumaga*. At its meetings the boys sat and spoke according to the ranking of their matai. Often they fished
together, dividing the catch equally. When the village fono
had a special celebration in mind such as a great wedding
or visiting trip, the aumaga built a community taro patch
to supply the occasion. They also prepared the chiefs' food
and defended the chiefs' honor. As a result they were
treated with some consideration and earned the right to become title bearers themselves in time.

In the past the young and untitled girls of the village had
had an organization known as the *aualuma* which waited
upon the village maiden. The aualuma now reappeared

only upon special occasions when a dance was held or guest houses had to be refurbished for important visitors. Its place has been taken by the Women's Committee.

I dropped in on a meeting of the Women's Committee which had been called to celebrate the monthly inspection of the district nurse. It was an impressive affair. All the members appeared in starched white uniforms with red collars and cuffs, bearing ample supplies of taro, sardines, Kool-Aid, and cake. The wives of chiefs duly arranged themselves at their appropriate posts while the untitled girls crowded in at the back. The wife of the highest chief was naturally chairman, and the wife of the highest talking chief welcomed the nurse. This took time. After these formalities there was a long period of friendly chatter, followed in the afternoon by the feast. Inspection of babies came somewhat as an afterthought, but they looked quite healthy in any case. Vai told me that the chiefs had been grumbling about the Women's Committee. It was too successful—hours were spent in pleasant chatter which might have been spent weeding the plantations. But the chiefs were hardly in a position to criticize, as far as I could see, and the Women's Committee continued to flourish.

But the most active organizations of all were the churches. Salani had two, a London Missionary Society, and a Methodist. Apparently one could be active in either or both. Almost every adolescent in the village seemed to be in one of the choirs and members could not miss rehearsal without a fine. Besides two services on Sunday and one on Wednesday, the women also had their church clubs. The Methodist women's club required a white uniform with blue collars and cuffs. The primary duty of its members was to keep the pastor's house well supplied with sheets, mats, and dishes, and to see that the pastor got the first basket of food from their ovens on Sunday. But they had more far-reaching responsibilities as well. Four times a year they marched off, in uniform, of course, to district or island meetings of the organization, and it was their steady coconut collections that made the Methodist cathedral in Apia possible.

For anyone who had time there were any number of weddings, funerals, christenings, church dedications, and cricket games sponsored by relatives up and down the coast. Obviously the mundane problem of earning a living was of minor importance compared with all this. No wonder they preferred department stores to taro plantations—it was easier to get food out of them.

Two days later we checked Salani's deed in the Apia land office. Sixteen thousand acres had been returned to Falealili District of which Salani is a part. No one had ever claimed any of this land, but if they ever did, distribution was to be made according to the "customs and usages of the Samoan people" by a group of chiefs known as the Falealili Land Committee and approved by the High Commissioner.

With this assurance we sailed back to Tutuila planning to return in six months to work with Salani and establish a plantation of our own.

CHAPTER EIGHT

Into the Forest Primeval

The next six months kept us very busy. Intrigued by the design of Samoan fales my engineer father designed a house for us, whose half louver, half screen walls combined the coolness of a fale with privacy from mosquitoes and black-eyed children. It was raftered to withstand a hurricane and inexpensive enough to fit our budget. We were delighted with it. We purchased most of it from the Sears, Roebuck catalogue—floor tile, roofing iron, plastic screen, hydraulic ram, wood stove, and kerosene refrigerator.

Chippy, our third child, was born into a world of crates, nails, and tins of tar. Six weeks later he was crated himself and loaded with five tons of house, furniture, fencing, and farm tools onto the same little boat that originally brought us to Tutuila. Our old pickup truck was lashed to the deck, to the inconvenience of all aboard.

I was so tired I have no recollection of whether the ride was rough or not. It probably was. In deference to our careening truck the passengers slept scrambled together on the rear hatch cover. At midnight while I was feeding the baby I made the acquaintance of my neighbor, a cheerful young Catholic priest as enthusiastic as ourselves about developing Samoan villages. Propped against the wheelhouse on the other side was a wiry little white-haired merchant who had spent his life in the islands building a prosperous store. For some time he listened to us with a tolerant smile. Finally he could stand it no longer.

"Look here, kids," he broke in, "I have lived here for fifty years and I've made my bit. Believe me, I know these people by now. The British tried, the Germans tried, New Zealand tried, and so did the United States, but no one yet has been able to get a Samoan to change a hair of his head. Why do you think they are still so Samoan after all these years? They say, 'Thank God you have come,' but just go back a week later and see how far you got. You kids have a lot to learn about Samoa if you think you are going to change their way of life."

His words plunged us into silence. I had a feeling he might be right.

At three in the morning we pulled alongside the Apia wharf. I was somewhat at a loss as to what to do with three babies and a crated house at that time of the morning. The customs officer wanted 45 per cent duty on the old pickup, the saw, the fence, and the house. It began to look as if Western Samoa didn't want farmers any more than it wanted public servants. So we told him to keep our equipment for the present and stumbled wearily down the street to Aggie Grey's.

Aggie has a large house which she opens for tourists. She also has a large heart which she opened for us.

"Just move right into the basement rooms," she said when we had roused her. "You can pay me in tomatoes when your garden comes in."

After two days of negotiation the Treasury agreed to release our pickup, and we planned a trip inland to stake out our homestead in the forest. On the way we stopped at the Land Survey Office for another map.

"There's something funny about that map you gave us last year," I complained to the survey officer. "It took us all day to walk four miles."

"You're quite right," he replied. "Just recently we got some aerial survey pictures and discovered this island is considerably wider than those old Germans thought it was. Come look at these pictures. Here is the Fagatoloa River."

He placed two pictures together and set a pair of lenses on top. I looked for a while at a meaningless jumble, then suddenly the mountains sprang up at me. It was exactly like looking down from a plane. Before long I located the tremendous gorge we had seen.

"This is a lot easier than walking," I told Vai, "and if you think we are going to put a bridge across that chasm to connect Salani land with the road, you had better go to M.I.T. and take an advanced course in civil engineering first."

"When I was a boy," Vai said, "an old chief and I found a spot in that canyon so narrow we could jump across. I'm sure of it."

"If you find a spot like that," laughed the surveyor, "let us know and we'll put a bridge across for you. It looks impossible to us."

Vai pushed the lenses up and down the river several times. The gorge looked like one huge ditch from mountaintop to ocean. Finally he stopped right above Sopoaga Falls.

"It might be here," he said. "This is either a bend in the river or the crack I am thinking about."

I looked again. Sure enough, for a short distance the river seemed to disappear. But it was hard to say why. It might have been the angle of the plane.

We left the children with a helpful aunt and started off for that spot.

Our first expedition was a failure. The road had been completed down to the coast, but it was a sea of mud.

Several miles beyond the Mafa Pass a huge forest tree had fallen across the ruts. It would have taken fifty men to move it. Reluctantly we turned back.

Several days later we tried again, armed with an axe. This time we were more successful. The new road, like the former track, came within a few feet of the gorge at one point. We left the pickup there and set off through the forest towards Sopoaga Falls. With a bush knife Vai cut our way through a mass of weeds and vines. For a while we lost the river and the gorge entirely, but a roaring sound through the forest indicated it was somewhere near. Then we caught a glimpse of the lip of the cataract and the swirling torrent plunging into the abyss below. It frightened me to look at it. Soon we were back in the woods again. A few minutes later we turned to scramble down a little bank. I could hear the river roaring somewhere but couldn't see it. I was about to run across the gully and up the other side when Vai suddenly shouted, "Stop!"

He sounded so urgent that I sat down. He rushed by me whacking at the vines beneath my feet. His knife uncovered a narrow dark crack in the rock at my very toes. I rolled over on my stomach and looked down. At first it seemed utter darkness, then I gradually discerned the roaring torrent sixty-five feet below tearing viciously between the narrow walls. Another jump and I would have been in it. As Vai cut the vines back we discovered that the crack was about ten feet wide with sides of solid black rock undercut with pot holes. Further upstream it widened slightly and the noise of the river became deafening. It seemed to be spewing steam at this point and we glimpsed a waterfall at least fifty feet high right inside the crack.

Vai shouted excitedly above the din, "This is it! I knew it was here! Look, if we cut down that big kava tree over there so that it falls across the crack, Falealili District will be connected with the road."

We found a perfect spot for a house on top of a knoll just north of the waterfall and in a grove of towering kava trees. We stood there and discussed how it would look three years from now with a house instead of a forest, and bananas instead of virgin timber as far as the eye could see.

The experience of my pioneer ancestors was so remote and the beauty of this place so tangible that I could envision nothing but pleasure at the prospect of living here. Having never seen a two-man saw in connection with a four-foot hardwood, or tried to hack a banana hole in a rooted forest floor, or made the acquaintance of the taro worm, I could think of nothing that might stand between us and success.

CHAPTER NINE

By What Right—?

Never in my wildest dreams had I imagined owning such a lovely piece of Mother Nature as Lafulemu with its whirlpools and waterfalls, delicate ferns, and giant hardwoods. But was "own" the right word for it? We didn't buy it. Nobody gave it to us. No one had lived here before. Whose was it to give, anyway? The situation bewildered me.

"Vai," I asked one evening at Aggie's, "who really does own the land on the east side of the river? I don't want to spend my life's savings building a home and find it isn't ours."

"Can't you stop thinking about 'owning' things," said Vai. "How many times have I told you that no one 'owns' things in Samoa. We only 'use' them. If we clear and plant this land it is ours. If we stop using it someone else can have it."

I pondered this concept of possession. Suppose someone else started "using" the land while we were still building our house? Or what would happen if we left to visit the States? Would we come back and find another family "using" our house and bananas?

"Can just anybody come along and start using it?" I queried.

"Of course not," said Vai. "Just anyone who belongs here. That land on the other side of the river belongs to Salani. I can use it because my people are from Salani. Salani and Lotofaga haven't yet decided which of them has the land on the side of the river where our house will be. But that makes no difference to us. I have relatives in Lotofaga too. So just stop worrying about it."

Next day we drove down to Lotofaga on the coast to visit our relatives. Lotofaga is a sandy village with few trees, but it is historically the seat of one of the four paramount chiefs. In commemoration of the fact that their matai had just been selected as mayor of the village, our relatives were building a new fale of some proportions. They showed it to us with pride. Unfortunately, however, they had run out of materials. The house had no floor. This was quite clearly an opportunity to cement our relationship with this branch of the family. Vai contributed five pounds to the cause. The matai had another problem as well. No sooner had he started his new fale than an even higher chief had started an even bigger fale right in his front yard. Vai agreed to propose the idea of town planning to the village fono.

Now that our matai was thoroughly convinced of the closeness of our relationship we explained that we also had a problem. We wanted to "use" that land by the waterfall to build a house. The mayor explained that in order to press their claim over Salani, the Lotofaga chiefs had divided the whole area back to the mountaintop among themselves. Fiti had been allotted the piece we had in mind. But this presented no particular difficulties. He called Fiti in to met us. Fiti was a smiling, good-natured fellow but he also had a problem. He wanted a gun for shooting pigeons in the forest. Vai agreed to help him solve this problem. Not to be outdone Fiti offered us the land by the waterfall providing the mayor would give him an even larger piece of land farther north. This the mayor was quite willing to do, since it would obviously relate him to our banana plantation. Our problems solved, we smiled and shook hands all around, delighted at the efficacy of Samoan kinship.

With this assurance we started our new house next day by felling a great kava tree on the knoll above the waterfall. We might capitalize our venture in the Samoan way, I learned, by buying the building materials on credit and convincing the carpenters of our close family ties. Once the building was completed we could arrange a great dedication ceremony to which all our relatives would have to contribute food, money, and fine mats. We could then give the money to the store, the fine mats to the carpenters, and the feast to the relatives. Everyone would be satisfied and we would have our house for nothing. Have entrepreneurs elsewhere ever devised such a simple and ingenious plan for raising capital? I turned down this opportunity, however. Not only did I question my own ability to organize a Samoan feast, but I also feared that too many people might then feel related to our bananas. Like a true palagi (European), I felt I was on firmer ground if I invested my own savings and a loan from my father in the venture.

Our choice of carpenters was a fortunate one. Pule had been trained by a well-known church builder and the U. S. Navy in Tutuila.

"This isn't a house, it's a boat," he commented after looking at my father's blueprint of a hurricaneproof roof bracing. Nevertheless, he and his thirteen boys erected it exactly as specified. In two weeks we had a cement platform, a tin roof and posts in between, but no walls, no rooms, no screens, and no plumbing.

"Now," said Vai, "it is time to move in." So we brought our household out from Apia by truck.

The next few weeks were a never-to-be-repeated experience in communal living. At the west end of the platform I set our primus stove on a crate. This composed the kitchen in which we prepared a stew of tinned sardines and pumpkin for never fewer than twenty-five people twice a day. At the other end of the platform we erected a barrier of packing cases to delineate our bedroom and furnished this area with mattresses on the floor for ourselves and two children, and a crib for the baby. The rest of the platform was dormitory for the fourteen carpenters, visitors, and our relatives from Lotofaga who had apparently decided to settle down with us. We had quite a few guests, all curious. When I opened my eyes in the morning I often found myself looking into a pair of solemn dark eyes staring through the mosquito netting.

Curiosity about our movable furnishings was also evident. Cases of food, tools, clothes, and sheets seemed to vanish from whichever direction I turned my back. Apparently they were being "used." Without walls, doors, or locks, I felt completely defenseless. I took to retrieving bits of my property from visitors' and carpenters' suitcases when they went to the river to bathe. I could see that our house would soon look like every other fale in Samoa, open, cool, neat as a pin—and devoid of furnishings.

Except for the mosquitoes which rose in clouds from the decaying forest floor and burned our ankles like grass fire, evening was a nostalgic part of the day. At dusk we all went down to the river for a leisurely bath in the cold, roaring torrent. Then came our lamplighting hour, and hour was no exaggeration. We had brought with us two impressive Coleman lanterns which gave a light like a 150-watt globe. Unfortunately, however, none of us knew how to light one. The directions called for kerosene, but we could not elicit a glimmer. Finally the head carpenter suggested gasoline. Even I could light that. For several nights our section of the forest glowed like Times Square. Then one

evening as I was demonstrating our new discovery to a visitor I unscrewed the wrong cap. The lamp went off like a flame thrower, burning out several days work of plastic screening and scaring us all speechless. After that we adopted little kerosene lamps with wicks and chimneys.

I soon became rather fond of those little lamps. They shed a cozy glow over the boys as we gathered for prayers each evening, and they did their best to cover the fact that we were having sardines for supper again. They absolutely precluded reading in bed so that I listened instead to the soft strumming and the rich harmony of our boys as they composed an endless song about the building of our house. Every evening the boys added another verse recounting the events of the day, and I invariably went to sleep forgiving them for all the little articles I had recovered from their suitcases, and thinking that there was no place where I would rather live than on a cement platform in the middle of a tropical rain forest.

My particular contribution to the house was the water tank. This was the only feature of the plan on which I grew to have a basic disagreement with my father. He felt that a metal tank would be difficult to make under the circumstances, so he designed a wooden one. He felt that to take full advantage of gravity it should be located on the roof. The carpenters built it accordingly. The difficulty was that no matter how carefully they fitted it, it leaked. Water spurted from its sides and bottom all over the kitchen.

Since I was the only one small enough to get inside it I was unanimously elected to the job of caulking. I spent the next few days with my ankles in the water and my head peering out over the red hot tin roof, stuffing putty into cracks that gained on me every day as the tank dried. I finished it off with a coat of sticky black tar and proudly called the boys to fill it with a lead from the hydraulic ram. It leaked as copiously as ever.

So I went to visit an old boat builder in Apia.

"Of course," he laughed, "the stuff you were putting in is water putty. Now you just watch me."

He twisted a strip of caulking deftly into a long crack, filled it with oil putty, and painted it over. It was tight as a drum. I thanked him, purchased the proper materials and returned to my tank. This time it wasn't so easy since it was already lined with soft warm tar. I stuck to everything and so did the caulking. When I did manage to get a twist through the tar and into the crack it just disappeared. I trebled and quadrupled the thread but it still went in out of sight. So I caulked it from the other side as well. Altogether I managed to get four balls of caulking and twelve pounds of putty into that tank. I tarred it again. It still leaked. So we finally settled the problem for good by making the space beneath it into a shower room.

We were so busy with the house we had no time for the plantation. Then one day Vai chopped down a tree so that it fell across the crack. We had connected Falealili District with the road. Vai ran blithely across the new bridge. But not I. It made me dizzy even to think of crossing that roaring chasm on a single log. So Vai continued on alone. In an hour he returned with a long face. Someone had taken the trouble to walk four miles back from Salani to cut a little strip through the jungle, about six feet wide and sixty feet long, right across the further end of our bridge. In the fa'aSamoa such a line indicates "use" and should not be crossed. In half an hour's time someone had deliberately severed our house from our plantation.

"That's silly," I cried. "Salani promised to help us. Why did someone come way back here to start a plantation when there are hundreds of untouched acres closer to the village?"

"That's not the point," said Vai. "No one intends to build a plantation here. Someone just wants to stop us. Remember that Samoan villages are a very delicate balance of power. If one family, like ours, starts a big new plantation it throws everyone's status out of line. Of course families not related to mine will try to stop us. When my brother started a plantation he crept out at night to fell trees. He cleared a claim of about three acres before someone crosscut him."

"Then Salani deserves to stay poor," I fumed. "Two thousand years and it hasn't even opened up one square mile of the richest land on earth. Why, in one tenth of that time my ancestors opened a continent! And now that blasted village wants to stop one person who does show some initiative. Doesn't it bother you?"

"Not in the least," laughed Vai blowing me a kiss, "you look cute when you get mad. Just sit tight, sweetheart, till I get back." And he swung off through the forest towards Salani.

"How did you get along?" I inquired anxiously when he returned that evening.

"Just fine," said Vai. "They offered me one thousand acres. We can start clearing tomorrow. In fact they volunteered to clear it for us. Want to read about it?" He tossed a sheet of paper on the bed.

I ran my eyes over the document.

"We, the chiefs and orators of Salani," it read, "agree to grant our native son exclusive right to clear any land north of the Sopoaga Creek and east of the dry Saili river bed for a period of seven years. He shall have exclusive right to the product of any land cleared and planted during this period and shall be entitled to pass this right on to his heirs so long as they keep this land under proper cultivation. Any land not cleared during this period or not maintained after this period shall revert to the village for redistribution."

The document was signed by every chief in the village but one.

"How did you do it?" I murmured with awe.

"Just a little psychology," he said. "You have to know how these boys think. Remember the deed we saw in Apia granting Falealili District sixteen thousand acres in return for loyalty during the Mau Rebellion? According to that deed the land was to be distributed 'according to the customs and usages of the Samoan people' by the Falealili Land Committee, with the approval of the High Commissioner. That deed was made in the 1920s. A committee was appointed and recommended that each Falealili village be granted the strip of land directly behind it. No one ever officially claimed any of the land, the committee members died, and were never replaced. The present High Commissioner now claims he has final authority. He feels this whole grant should be leased by the government to any landless Samoan whether he comes from Falealili or not. I just pointed out to Salani that it would be far better for them to settle the land behind the village with their own people, rather than wait for the High Commissioner to lease it to strangers. They were so much in agreement that they wanted me to take the whole thing. Instead, I suggested we all start plantations back here, allotting each family a portion with a seven-year protection from crosscutting. They were only too happy to sign my agreement as a model. Maybe it gave them enough of a scare so they will start to develop it themselves, who knows?"

In the middle of the night I sat up in bed and prodded Vai awake.

"I just had an awful thought," I said. "What if the High Commissioner really does have final say? Your agreement

with Salani wouldn't mean a thing. He could move anyone on here anyway."

"For Pete's sake," groaned Vai. "Can't you ever relax?
The government couldn't move a stranger into Falealili
without starting a revolution here. By the time the government thinks of us again we will have lived here for fifty
years and will have this place by seniority, anyway. So just
keep still and go to sleep."

But my palagi mind just could not rest until that piece
of land was signed, sealed, and deposited in an archive
somewhere. I simply couldn't grasp the idea of really having
something without legally owning it.

Since I couldn't arouse Vai on the subject I finally took
matters into my own hands and consulted the Attorney
General. There must be some legal way to do it.

"You are breaking new ground," he warned me, "if you
insist on security of tenure. I have no precedent to go on.
But I will take a look at that government deed and Vai's
agreement with Salani."

A few days later he called me in.

"The deed says that the land should be held 'according
to the customs and usages of the Samoan people,'" he said.
"Vai's agreement is consistent with Samoan custom and
the Salani chiefs concur, so why don't you just file it in
the government archives and forget about it?"

I passed Vai's agreement in to the appropriate office but
it was hardly forgotten about. In four hours it was on the
High Commissioner's desk and Vai was on the carpet.

"Just where did this strange document come from?" the
High Commissioner asked in an icy voice. Vai gave me a
look that indicated exactly what he thought of women in
politics, but he replied evenly to the High Commissioner.

"We are honestly bewildered as to how to go about se-
curing a piece of my ancestral land. We would appreciate
knowing just how it should be done."

The High Commissioner showed us a typewritten copy of the deed.

"It says here that I should approve claims upon recommendation of the Falealili Land Committee. Apply to me for a lease and I will reappoint the Falealili Land Committee and forward it to them."

"Does the Falealili Land Committee agree that leases are 'in accordance with the customs and usages of the Samoan people?'" I asked.

"The deed mentions nothing about Samoan customs and usages," he replied. I searched his copy of the deed. The words were nowhere to be found.

"Well," said Vai to cover my embarrassment, "it doesn't really matter to us whether we have a lease or a grant, so long as we have some security for our plantation."

"Then write me an application," said the High Commissioner.

Outside I asked Vai, "Didn't that deed we saw last year mention 'the customs and usages of the Samoan people'? The Attorney General thought it did."

"I thought I saw it too," said Vai. "But if you really want to know we would have to check at the Lands and Titles Office again."

We did. But the original deed was nowhere to be found.

In due course the Falealili Land Committee was reconstituted. At its one and only meeting it granted us 250 acres of Falealili land.

A week later the High Commissioner presented us with the terms of a lease—twenty years renewable for twenty, five shillings per acre per year retroactive to the time we came.

Vai scratched his head. "See what comes of your big mouth," he said. "If I do sign this lease every chief in Falealili will be after my scalp for agreeing to rent our own land. Plenty of people, including the Minister of Lands himself, have opened plantations on this land, but no one was ever stupid enough to ask for it until you came along. Now you figure out what to do next."

We sent the High Commissioner a counterproposal suggesting that the Falealili Land Committee approve an economic development plan for the whole area, giving preference to persons from Falealili, and using rents for the development of roads and water. We offered to sign a lease at five shillings per acre, providing the Falealili Land Committee itself approve the lease idea, and other persons using the land came under the same arrangement.

The High Commissioner's reply was prompt and incisive. He had never heard of a prospective tenant suggesting the terms of a lease. Thereupon the issue was settled in true Samoan fashion. No one ever mentioned it again—least of all, myself.

CHAPTER TEN

Stone Wheels

I once read the story of Mr. O'Keefe, an enterprising young man who found himself shipwrecked among the easygoing Yap Islanders. After some investigation he discovered one item for which they would expend time, productive effort, and indeed their very lives. What they wanted above all else were great stone wheels carved by hand from the cliffs of an island two hundred miles away. By providing transportation and cutting tools in return for *bêche de mer*, O'Keefe made his fortune.

Unfortunately Samoans do not go in for stone wheels. It took us some time to discover what our neighbors did prize enough to induce them to help us clear a hundred acres of forest. I must admit right here that nothing on earth would have induced me personally to face that gigantic tangle with only two arms, one axe, and a saw. But since that was all we had, I trusted that Samoans were made of sterner stuff.

In my limited experience most people worked for money. Not our neighbors. They had no objection to money, but with breadfruit and relatives everywhere it was something they could easily do without.

During our first few weeks we had plenty of helpers but a 100 per cent turnover.

"Look here," I said to Vai, as the truth began to dawn, "these boys aren't coming here for the pay, they just want to see what's going on. When the general curiosity is satisfied we just won't have any workers."

"Well, can you blame them?" asked Vai. "All they get out of it personally is the food, since cash usually goes to the matai. But that gives me an idea. Maybe we could get steadier work if we encouraged the young men to bring their families. If they weren't so obligated to the matai they could use their pay to raise their own standard of living."

Two days later we adopted Mo'e, not a day over twenty, and his wife Ata, not a day under forty. If we had figured that their physiological condition might limit the number of their dependents we were wrong. Within the week they had settled in six adopted children and two maiden aunts. On Saturday noon each week they left us, taking with them four huge baskets of our taro for the "old folks at home."

"Family life is no stone wheel," I told Vai. "It's only a stone around the neck. Think of something else."

"Well, let's try Salani next," suggested Vai. "Remember? They wanted a co-op."

I remembered various things about co-ops.

On Sunday after church we were sitting cross-legged in a circle of Salani chiefs, eating fish and taro with our fingers. Dinner after church is a leisurely communal meal, a time for talk and laughter. Vai regaled them with stories about America.

Finally he leaned back against his post.

"Do you remember that co-op store we discussed last year?" he asked. "Did you ever collect the five hundred pounds in shares to start it?"

We were not particularly surprised to learn that ours had been the only share collected and that the treasurer had resigned. It would have been surer to borrow it, the chiefs pointed out.

"Well, I have an even better way to get it," said Vai. "I will give you five pounds an acre for clearing my plantation. Then I will have a plantation, you will have a co-op, and we will all be protecting the land for Salani."

The chiefs were enthusiastic about this all-encompassing solution. They decided to call up their young men's organization, the aumaga. They assured us that in a week one hundred acres would be cleared.

"Are you sure you know how big an acre is?" I asked surprised.

"Of course we know," the high chief replied scornfully. "Are you doubting the strength of our young men?"

The village agreed to provide taro and bananas for the workers if we contributed sardines and transportation. The project was to commence on Monday morning.

At 6 A.M. Monday we parked our truck across the river from Salani. The village was ready. Matai, of course, went first—two loads of them complete with suitcases. Then four loads of young men with knives and axes—about sixty-five persons in all. Clearly this was to be a great affair.

It was noon before the last load arrived. Six of the young men prepared an oven. The rest built an enormous lean-to of logs and leaves in our front yard. Matai, of course, were to sleep in our house.

Upon completion of these labors there was just time for a bath in the river, evening prayers, the evening meal, and a crayfish hunt in the river.

Next morning the matai met in council and, using many Biblical admonitions, instructed the young men in their duties for the week. Vai led the boys across the bridge and showed them where to commence cutting. The matai, of course, stayed in the house to deliberate upon the founding of the co-op store.

It took forty-eight cans of sardines a day to feed the men of Salani, the major portion of them going to the matai, who ate first. After the second day it seemed to my suspicious eye that the number of young men had dwindled, though the consumption of sardines remained the same.

"Oh, it's hard to tell," said Vai, "they are all scattered through the forest."

But he checked the lean-to that night. About fifteen boys were present. When he mentioned this to the matai they assured him that the married men had returned to Salani for the night and would be back before dawn.

Saturday was the day for measurement of the week's clearing. The matai were afraid the boys might have slightly exceeded their one hundred acres but we agreed to pay for any overage. Then in stately procession Vai led them across the log to measure what the aumaga had cleared.

From somewhat disjointed accounts I gathered later that the matai had some difficulty locating not only the clearing but also the young men. Eventually they found two pigeon hunters who pointed out where the aumaga had been working earlier in the week. Total clearing: 3¾ acres.

"That eliminates co-ops as a stone wheel," I commented after we had deposited the last matai back in Salani. "Those boys went right back home through the woods and stayed there."

"Well, at least it should prove to you doubting Westerners that the matai are not in a position to exploit their young men," said Vai.

"Their bargaining power must be terrific," I laughed, "if they can walk off the job like that. It's obvious we will have to find a wheel that appeals to the young men as well as to their matai. What moved you to action when you were young?"

"Girls and teachers," Vai replied promptly. "And that gives me an idea. Let's turn our plantation into a farm school like the one I went to in Hawaii. We could get any number of boys that way."

Relieved that he hadn't seized upon the other angle, I tentatively agreed. "We might offer courses in general science, poultry raising, and bananas, if we could find a book about it," I suggested.

"If that's what you intend to teach," said Vai flatly, "you'll never get a single student. You have to teach them what they want to know—English and typing."

"English and typing!" I cried. "That's ridiculous. These boys don't hear English spoken once in ten years, and they never saw a typewriter."

"But that's what they want," Vai insisted. "If you don't believe me, just ask them. And there's no use waiting around about this. School will start day after tomorrow."

Apparently Vai had no trouble finding pupils. The health inspector had closed Salani's school for lack of sanitary facilities. When Salani heard of Vai's idea they immediately proposed that we take over its entire educational program. We were well qualified, since we had the only septic tank on the south coast of Upolu. But Vai refused on the grounds that ours was to be a farm school for adolescent boys only.

It would be a stretch of the imagination to call some of the boys who appeared on Wednesday morning adolescent. Some could hardly have experienced ten summers. It would also be stretching it to say that they all had an insatiable thirst for knowledge. Some were merely investigating whether our food was better than the fare at home. It would even be incorrect to say that they were all boys. Several were girls. Some did not stay for the "practical" sessions at all but appeared only for meals and classes in the evening.

The first evening was an orientation session. I was speedily oriented to the fact that they really did want English and typing. What was their aim in life? They told me quickly—to become store clerks in Apia.

Typing was out since my typewriter was broken. I couldn't teach banana culture since they knew more about it than I did. So I settled on general science. Vai took English grammar, a topic I could never understand.

As an educational experience the school was a success. I learned a lot. As a stone wheel it was a flop.

"You don't really expect these little fellows to chop down those enormous trees?" I asked Vai. "Why, their parents would have us in for child labor."

"Their parents wouldn't mind a bit," replied Vai, "but unfortunately we aren't their parents. Put them to making a vegetable garden. I'll have to think of something else for the bush."

A few weeks later a solution walked right up our driveway. The matai of Falevao village came to consult Vai about a serious problem. They had to have a new house for their pastor before the annual church convention, but a ruthless storekeeper had cut off their credit. Would Vai loan them the money?

Vai knew a stone wheel when he saw one.

"Sorry," he said. "I have no money. But I'll tell you a secret. My wife has plenty. But she is a hard woman, a palagi, you know. I am sure she would never loan you a cent of it. But she does like bananas. I think she would pay you five pounds an acre if you cleared a little plantation for her."

Ten startled black eyes turned to look at me. Not having understood a word of the conversation, I smiled encouragingly and nodded my head.

"But we need the money right away," began the high chief, turning back to Vai.

"Be careful," Vai warned him. "Don't get her angry or she might drop the idea entirely."

They looked at me again. I gave a nod and they signed an agreement for twelve acres, pay upon completion.

I have nothing but admiration for the five young men of Falevao who appeared for work next day. From dawn to dark they battled the dripping forest giants, lost in a tangle of vines and flying buttresses. After four days, ten strong arms and five sharp axes emerged victorious. Twelve acres looked as if the wrath of God had breathed upon them. They had become an impenetrable graveyard of fallen trunks and battered branches, open to the blinding sun.

"What a terrible thing," I choked, and burst into tears.

"Well, I'll be darned," exclaimed Vai in astonishment. "I thought you wanted a banana plantation."

By trial and error we had begun to uncover the stone wheels of Samoa. Wages, co-ops, and worldly wisdom captured interest but for a day. It was church buildings, large and imposing, that commanded real strength in those brown arms and commitment in those carefree hearts.

CHAPTER ELEVEN

Sturm und Drang

Before long I had cause to recall again Margaret Mead's theory that because of their easy premarital habits Samoan young people are spared our Western period of adolescent "storm and stress." After a few direct observations on the subject, I began to wonder. If they didn't have any *sturm und drang* about it, I certainly did.

My first experiences involved a long series of young ladies who came to help me take care of the house and children. My first assistant just appeared one day. She said her name was Lele and that she had been sent by our relative in Lotofaga to help with the housework. She couldn't have been more than fourteen but she had muscles like an Indian. Delighted, I handed her my bucket and brush and set her to work scrubbing our asphalt tile floor. She approached the task with vigor. When I returned she was sitting in a pool of water, pulling up the loosened tiles and scrubbing the cement beneath for good measure.

She was especially eager to demonstrate her muscular prowess to our school boys. When I discovered Vai's blue jeans rent exactly in two, the boys informed me that Lele had been demonstrating wood chopping under the clothesline.

Her strength failed her, however, when I sent her to the river to wash clothes. When I inquired about the diapers she told me the river had snatched them right out of her hand and taken them over the waterfall.

"What you need," said Vai, "is a housegirl with recommendations. I will ask my sisters to send someone."

Two of Vai's sisters were pastors' wives. Many village girls were sent to them for "protection" and training. Each sister sent me a promising candidate.

Fili was sixteen and rather retiring. She would be scared to death of boys, I told myself hopefully. Tina was exactly the opposite. She gave everyone orders—including myself—and backed them with so robust a figure that we all obeyed. If the boys were half as scared of her as I was, she was perfectly safe, I figured. I made her foreman of the vegetable garden and she practically made it self-supporting.

A few weeks later Tavita joined us. He was seventeen, with curly hair and an open, smiling face, well named, indeed, after the shepherd boy of the psalms. He was soon the star of our evening classes.

Life proceeded cheerfully enough. Already I could detect development among our protégées, especially Fili.

"Look at her," I said proudly to Vai. "A week ago she wouldn't say a word, now she shrieks and giggles all the time."

"So I notice," said Vai with a frown. That night he locked all the doors of our house. The girls always slept in the house with us.

In the middle of the night I sat up in bed with a start. The house and forest were still as a graveyard. I must have been dreaming, I thought to myself, and went to sleep again.

The same experience occurred several times during the next few weeks, but I could never quite put my finger on what wakened me. The click of a bolt, the squeak of a door, the brush of a lavalava? Finally one night I got up and went out to the front door. It was unlocked. I looked for the girls. Fili was gone.

When I asked her about it next morning she was incensed. She had not moved all night and if I meant to impugn her reputation she would only be too glad to return to my sister-in-law. I began to wonder if I was just getting nervous.

Two weeks later Fili's personality took a change for the worse. Her giggles suddenly disappeared and her face became expressionless. She seemed to be living in a different world. She took clothes to wash in the morning and wandered home late in the afternoon with her bundle untouched.

One Sunday, Ula, our youngest pupil, came running in gibbering with excitement. He gasped something to Vai and they both ran out. Ten minutes later they returned with Fili who was practically in a catatonic state.

"What's the matter with her?" I cried, alarmed.

"She was just about to jump into the waterfall," said Vai, calmly, and sat her down on the couch.

Two minutes later she was sobbing out a tale of woe to Vai. She was pregnant and Tavita refused to marry her. Vai called Tavita, but he only shook his curly head. If Fili were pregnant, which he doubted, it was certainly not his fault, he insisted. It was just a ruse to get him to marry her.

Unable to get any clearer explanation Vai sent them both home. A few days later Tavita was back. I looked into his happy, innocent eyes that evening in class. Surely he could never have done a thing like that.

Next day Fili's parents came to call. They were irate. Hadn't they sent Fili to us for protection? What kind of a home did we have, anyway? It was up to us to see that she got properly married. I was covered with embarrassment. But we couldn't move Tavita. Fili ended up by marrying a more agreeable young man at home.

"Tina," I said to my robust foreman as I reassigned her to housework, "let's make an agreement. If you ever want to get married just let me know ahead of time. I'll make you a three-story wedding cake. But it must be on the up and up."

"Ho!" she roared. "Do you think I care about boys?"

"I hope not," I muttered softly.

As soon as I brought her back to work in the house Tina's personality changed too. Her bumptious spirit disappeared and she became as shy and retiring as Fili had been.

"I'm glad she doesn't giggle, anyway," I told Vai, "because that is a terrible sign."

"People differ," said Vai thoughtfully.

Saturday night Vai and I drove to Apia to the movies.

"We'll be back tomorrow," Vai told them. I asked Tina to go with us but she refused. She had to look after things, she insisted, and would lock herself inside the house.

After the movie, Vai was restless. "Let's go home tonight," he said. "I have a peculiar feeling."

Having great respect for Vai's intuition I readily agreed. By 2 A.M. we were coasting down the mountain towards Lafulemu. Instead of turning in the driveway, Vai snapped off the lights and parked on the main road.

"Come with me," he whispered.

We crept by the boys' fale. It was empty. We moved on to our own house and peeked in. The living room floor was covered with bodies. The moonlight revealed two figures asleep in our bed.

Vai snapped on his flashlight. There was a sudden commotion inside. Tina sat up in our bed rubbing her eyes. The figure beside her vanished. In a high temper Vai stormed into the house.

"Just what are you doing in our house?" he roared to the boys.

Tavita sat up sleepily on the floor. "Tina was frightened here alone," he said. "So we put her in your bed and slept out here to protect her."

Vai counted the protectors. They were all on the floor. Had we been seeing things again?

Next evening at prayers Vai talked to them like a father about the structure of a happy family. Tavita read the scripture and Tina led the hymns; they seemed like simple and sincere children. I felt quite ashamed of my suspicions of the previous night.

Next morning Tina was gone, together with a suitcase, several sheets, two pillows, and a towel. Vai ran to the boys' house and counted them quickly. One was missing—Tavita.

Clearly Samoan premarital habits were beyond me. Vai sent for his sister to handle this one. She assured me that such elopements, though common in Samoa, were not considered in keeping with Christian doctrine. As a pastor's wife in charge of young ladies, she must insist that Tavita and Tina get married. The only trouble was that no one could find them.

After several weeks they were discovered living in the forest behind Falevao. By that time, however, neither of them wanted to get married.

"For goodness' sake, let them go in peace," I proposed. "Just be thankful they know what they don't want."

"No," said Vai's sister firmly. "We must protect your reputation as having a Christian home. You provide the wedding cake and I will look for a dress. The wedding will be next Saturday."

It wasn't exactly in line with our original agreement, but I iced a three-story wedding cake for Tina and sent it to Falevao by bus on Saturday morning. In the evening the returning bus dropped me a note,

We decided not to get married this week, but thank you for the wedding cake. It was very good. Please send another for our wedding next Saturday.

Tina and Tavita

The *sturm und drang* affected more than adolescents. Nunu was our best worker. He was a wiry little fellow about thirty-five years old. He worshiped Vai, worked like a demon, and was always happy and eager as a child. God had spared Nunu some of life's temptations by making him deaf and dumb from birth.

Vai and Nunu had known each other since childhood. They conversed by the hour in a sign language all their own. Nunu didn't care about pay, but Vai was saving it for him to buy a hearing aid.

One evening Nunu came in with shining eyes. He was never sad, but I had never seen him so radiant. With a few movements of his hands he told Vai that he was about to get married.

Vai was delighted. "Who's the lucky lady?" his fingers inquired.

"Mo'e's aunt," signaled Nunu. "She is going to bear me a son."

Vai's face fell. The lady in question was somewhat more than an aunt to Mo'e, and the baby, if there was one, could not possibly have been Nunu's. It was obviously time for Vai to explain to Nunu about the birds and the bees.

Such explanations are delicate in any language—but in sign language they are impossible. Vai's hands were tongue-tied and I doubled up with laughter. Nunu looked at us innocently and laughed too. He was delirious with happiness.

"Maybe you had better explain it to the lady instead," I suggested.

Vai called in Sali. She was a hard-bitten woman of uncertain age who looked as if even her mother hadn't loved her. She was polite but firm. Nothing we could say could make her change her mind. If Nunu couldn't spend his savings, she could show him how. Nunu watched her with adoration. The wedding was set for Saturday.

On Tuesday I fired Mo'e. He had beaten his wife into an apparent state of insensibility. Somewhat to my surprise she revived in time to leave with him. They went off with the new shoes Nunu had proudly purchased for his wedding and hidden in the ceiling.

Next day our youngest student came panting into the kitchen. "Come quickly," he called. "Mo'e has kidnaped Sali."

"Kidnaped her?" I asked, surprised. "How could he? He isn't even here."

"But I saw him," insisted Ula. "He came and took her by the arm while we were weeding bananas. They have gone off down the road."

I couldn't imagine Sali being taken anywhere involuntarily. But I could imagine some repercussions. My first inclination, as in all such situations, was to call Vai. But unfortunately he had gone to Apia.

"Run, call Nunu," I told Ula. After all it was up to Nunu to defend his own.

In no time at all Nunu came tearing out of the bush, his kindly face black with rage. Brandishing a bush knife, he leaped into the back of the pickup.

I held out my hand for the knife. But he refused. Hiding my trembling knees, I signaled—no knife, no ride.

His hands clenched and the muscles rippled up and down his arm. After a long moment he gave me the knife. I threw it into the grass and hopped into the car. We started down towards Lotofaga at full speed. Along the way we met people who laughed understandingly and waved us on down the road. News did get around.

A mile beyond Lotofaga we caught up with the escaping pair. As I screeched to a halt, Sali dived for the ditch and Nunu leapt from the back of the car like a cat. Before I could reach him he had his hands around Mo'e's neck as if to choke him.

"Stop it!" I shouted as if he could hear, and wrenched his arm away.

"Where are you taking Sali?" I asked Mo'e as soon as I could straighten out my voice. Mo'e's face was white as a ghost. His lips moved but no words came out.

I went to the ditch and dragged Sali to her feet. The sight of her face restored my confidence. She was obviously even more frightened than I was. I put on a brave front.

"It's up to you, anyway," I said shaking her. "Just decide right now. Are you going with Mo'e or Nunu?"

She collapsed on the road with a wail. I shook her again.

"Stop bawling," I shouted in my best Samoan. "Nunu won't hurt you. Just make up your mind in a hurry."

Nunu stepped towards her, and Mo'e, finding himself free, darted off down the road like a bird, leaving his lady-love behind. Sali took one look at each of them and ran after Mo'e.

Nunu looked after her, dumbfounded. I touched his arm.

"Good riddance," I whispered softly, but he didn't move. After a long moment he suddenly spat. I spat too. He looked at me, comforted, and we climbed back into the car.

Vai came home late that night and I told him the story.

"Hooray," he said with a whistle of relief. "Let's go down and congratulate Nunu."

Nunu's fale was dark, but two heads were rolled up in his lavalava. Sali had changed her mind.

A few weeks after our successful bush clearing with Falevao, the chiefs of Lefaga approached us. They wanted to build a schoolhouse, and offered to clear twenty acres of land if we would deposit one hundred pounds to their account with the Education Department. Vai agreed. He introduced me to the paramount chief.

"Chief Toelau," he said, "is famous for having had more wives than any other chief in Samoa."

I congratulated Toelau. He was wrinkled, lame, and toothless, but there was definitely a twinkle in his eye.

The workers from Lefaga arrived next day, thirty strapping youths from Lefaga's young men's society. Vai was just giving them directions for cutting when another chief from Falevao came up the driveway leading twenty girls. It was the young women's organization of Falevao coming to weed taro.

A look of consternation crossed Vai's face when he saw them.

"Oh, no!" he muttered in English, "and me a pastor's son."

It was a few minutes before I could catch him alone.

"What's the matter?" I inquired anxiously.

"An *aumoega*," he answered grimly.

"What's that?"

"A big Samoan party when a young men's group visits a young women's group. Toelau knows all about it," sighed Vai. "But I have done my best. I told Toelau there were to be absolutely no parties on this plantation. I put the boys in the large fale way down by the waterfall. The girls will have to sleep in the garage next to our bedroom."

I was a bit disappointed myself, for a little party might be fun.

But when Vai and I returned from our evening bath, the party was already in progress in the garage. Everyone was there laughing and singing and clapping for the swaying siva dancers. The boys' group sang and danced a few numbers, then the girls did the same. Items of entertainment shifted back and forth between them with never an awkward pause. Sometimes they recited poems and everyone rocked with laughter.

"What's wrong with this?" I whispered to Vai. "A little recreation will lift everyone's morale."

Vai shrugged his shoulders.

Towards midnight both sides produced their comic dancers. Fat old women jumped and bumped and ground, to everyone's great delight.

"Time for us to retire," whispered Vai.

Since our house had no walls, just louvers and screens, sleep was out of the question. I lay in bed listening to the music and laughter until dawn.

The sun was well up when I woke. The garage was still, but someone was pounding on the door. When I opened it a Falevao chief rushed in to Vai. After a hurried conference Vai came out.

"Call in the matai of Lefaga," he ordered one of our boys sharply. "Five Falevao women are missing."

Work stopped for the day as the Lefaga chiefs sat in a circle on our living room floor and deliberated. Four of the elopements caused no concern. The girls were single and would be back in a few days. But the fifth was a poser. The lady was married, to a high chief at that. Wars have been fought for lesser reasons.

The only solution, the chiefs decided, was an *ifoga*—a ceremonial apology. Lefaga villagers would spend the next few days collecting pigs and fine mats from relatives along the coast. On Friday they would present these to the village of Sapo'e where the injured husband was visiting and ask his forgiveness.

Everyone agreed that this was the only thing to be done and Sapo'e was notified so that it could provide a suitable reception for repentant Lefaga.

As news of the ifoga ceremony spread up the coast several of the eloped couples returned to join the festivities, and relatives gathered from nearby villages. Work ceased.

Early Friday morning we trucked the boys down to the edge of the village where they formed a long procession. The chiefs came first holding fine mats over their heads. The young men followed with whole pigs, kegs of beef, and baskets of taro.

The procession crossed the village square in complete silence and sat down humbly in front of the house where the injured husband was residing. He sat inside without turning his head as if completely unaware of their existence. The sun rose directly overhead and beat down fiercely on the bare backs in front of the house. Still no one moved or spoke. The sun started down again. The people inside the house began to stir. I could see they were getting hungry. The injured man turned his head very slightly, just enough to count the fine mats out of the corner of his eye. Suddenly he rose and went to the front of the house. He beckoned the chiefs inside. They were forgiven. War would not ensue.

The mood of the occasion changed in a flash. The fine mats were presented with oratory. There was kava and the young men gaily heaped food mats and baskets for their chiefs.

As evening settled down it was Sapo'e's turn to honor its Lefaga guests. It presented them, in turn, with enough food to last for a week. Finally Sapo'e's young women appeared for the evening entertainment. There was much laughter. Rollicking song and dance items passed from side to side and it all seemed vaguely familiar. At midnight Yai and I excused ourselves and drove home to a very quiet plantation.

Next morning we were again awakened by pounding on the door. A Sapo'e chief rushed in with indignation written in every wrinkle of his brow. Eight Sapo'e girls were missing!

CHAPTER TWELVE

My Matai

Vai was only a young man himself. He had no title. In the extraordinary flexibility of Samoan custom, he sat with the chiefs because of his education. But that did not make him a matai. Several families tried to bestow their titles upon him but he always refused.

"Haven't I got enough worries as it is?" he said, "with a Western wife, three children, a farm school, and the plantation? What if we had thirty more mouths to feed and goodness knows how many feasts to take care of?"

I shuddered.

"And besides," he continued, "where would this plantation be if I spent every day at village council meetings like a good matai?"

I heartily agreed that he should remain a young man forever in view of the burdens of mataiship.

It was Vai's old uncle who disagreed. Apa could not have differentiated a Pontiac from a potato, but he was infinitely wise in the ways of Samoans.

"My son," he told Vai in his fatherly way, "what will happen to the Samoan way of life if its educated young men refuse to take titles? And what will happen to our family? The best of your father's family became pastors. The best of your own family have gone abroad and many have not returned. Where are the proud sons of Toa whose power extended from the reef to those mountaintops? Our family will crumble unless it has good leadership.

"As a young man without a title you are nothing. Someday you may have to rent this land your forefathers discovered from a stranger in Apia, and scratch it selfishly for yourself like a Westerner.

"But as a matai you would be everything. Land goes with the title. A family and a village would stand behind you, and your voice would be heard. Young men are the muscle of Samoa, but the matai are always its brain.

"It is in my power to grant you the Fuima title of Salani, one of the highest in Falealili District. I want you also to take the Amitu title in the village of Lotofaga which will give our family influence on the east side of the river."

As Apa well knew, Vai had a weakness for the tribal line of reasoning. He cared about his family and he cared about Samoa. Apa went home with Vai's promise and my best blanket to warm his aging bones.

"Do you think you could be a *faletua?*" Vai asked, eyeing me sceptically.

"What's that?" I inquired.

"A *faletua* is the wife of a matai. It comes from the words *fale* (house) and *tua* (back) and means she stays in the back of the house to direct the household, organize feasts, and see that there are enough tapas for ceremonies and sleeping mats for guests. She directs the work of the women in the plantation and on the reef. When the matai is away she speaks for him. She is the fountainhead of knowledge on family genealogies and custom. Above all, she welcomes all guests with a smile no matter how many sardines are, or are not, in the pot." He looked at me significantly.

"I guess not," I said sadly, thinking of my deficiencies in all these lines. "I couldn't possibly make a good faletua."

"That's too bad," said Vai, shaking his head, "because you are my wife already. You will just have to learn. You can begin by organizing my *saofa'i*. I'll get my mother and sisters to help you."

"What is a saofa'i?" I asked as a starter.

"When a family has selected its matai," explained Vai, "it must present him formally to the village for approval. The village council offers him a cup of kava to show that he is acceptable to the group. Then he must provide a feast for the village."

"A feast for all of Salani?" I asked in an appalled whisper.

"No," he said, "feasts for both Salani and Lotofaga. I am taking titles in both of them. We will need at least five cows."

"Cows cost forty pounds each," I whispered.

"Stop giving me such ridiculous arguments," snapped Vai. "Are you going to be my faletua or not?"

I never did discover what other faletuas did under such circumstances. In my own case, I thought of the enormous tuna fish we used to sell in the Pago co-op. They weighed almost as much as a cow and cost a lot less. With the help of fifty dollars and a relative I purchased ten enormous fish, totaling about 1500 pounds, direct from the Japanese fishermen. I ordered them sent to Apia on the inter-island boat.

Vai was impressed with his faletua and we drove to Apia to escort the fish home. The boat docked at one-thirty in the morning, as usual, and the wharf was covered with people. Our fish were wheeled off and the crowd formed a large circle around them, ohing and ahing about what the Samoan seas could produce.

"One . . . two . . . three . . . four . . . five . . . six . . . seven . . . eight . . . nine . . . ten," they chanted as the bodies piled up.

"That's it," said Vai cheerfully. "You keep an eye on them while I take these papers to the captain."

"I'd like to see anyone tote one of those great slippery things away," I laughed, and turned back to admire them.

One . . . two . . . three . . . four . . . five . . . six . . . seven . . . eight . . . nine . . . ! There were only nine of them! I counted again.

"Vai," I shouted, "one of our fish has got away!"

Vai was furious. "I thought I told you to watch them," he said, making his way back through the crowd.

"I did," I insisted, "I never took my eyes off them."

Vai made inquiries around the ogling circle. No, no one had seen a fish escaping. The captain assured us again that he had landed ten.

"Tuna can't fly!" fumed Vai. "Someone must have seen him go. Where is the policeman?"

That official was nowhere to be found.

Sadly, we hoisted nine fish into the pickup and started home. Just outside Apia we passed a taxi. Its rear spring had broken and the driver was sitting on the grass with his ukulele waiting for help.

"Look!" I called to Vai as we slowed down. An enormous tail was sticking out of the trunk of the taxi.

Vai jumped down and pulled the passenger bodily from the rear seat of the taxi. He was about to administer some physical discipline, when he suddenly stopped. It was the policeman!

Apa apparently had no trouble lining up the sixteenth Fuima title for Vai. All it required was his consent. But the Amitu title in Lotofaga was a different matter. This honor had to be approved by a whole family. One of our relatives had this title in mind for his own son, so the family called a meeting at the mayor's house in Lotofaga to discuss the situation. "Why don't we both be Amitu," proposed Vai to the assembled relatives. He was thinking of the other fifteen Fuimas. But one of the uncles objected.

"It's Vai or nothing," he said slapping his leg. Relations

in the family meeting became strained and talk grew tense. I saw several wives slip knives under their husband's mats. Alas, I had failed as a faletua. I had left my weapons at home.

Fortunately, open warfare did not break out. But the meeting went on and on. As the sun went down next day, Vai stood up and delicately sniffed the air.

"My fish," he said. "I am afraid I will have to give them all to Salani tomorrow or they will spoil."

That settled it. Two Amitu were presented to the village fono for approval, and we prepared for the feasts.

True to his word, Vai had sent for his largest and most capable sister, Taligi, to help with the saofa'i.

"Remember," he wrote her, "my wife is American. We must keep things simple for her sake. So don't bring any fine mats or talking chiefs with you."

But Taligi was in no mood to see her brother limited to a second-class celebration. Three days before the occasion she had arrived with two talking chiefs, five fine mats, two cases of sardines, a tin of hard tack, and a retinue from the village of Paia.

Vai dismissed the school and established the guests in the boys' house with Taligi in charge.

"Now," said Taligi, bustling into the kitchen with a broad smile, "don't worry about a thing. I'll tell you exactly what to do. Tonight we must present the talking chiefs with a *sua*."

"What's a *sua*?"

"A *sua* is a special ceremonial meal for chiefs," she explained, "and it always includes the same food: a scraped coconut, a roast pig, a bundle of taro, and a tapa cloth to cover it."

"What about a tuna fish," I suggested. "We don't have any pigs."

"A tuna wouldn't be a *sua*," she said firmly. "The only possible substitute for a pig is a barrel of beef. Then tomorrow for breakfast we must give them a ceremonial breakfast consisting of quarter loaves of toasted bread; these can be bought in burlap sacks from the bakery in Apia. It is always served with jam."

During the next two days more people arrived. By the eve of the festivities we had at least fifty relatives, all thoroughly versed in Samoan custom. Before dawn on the great day, Vai prodded me awake. Taligi was with him and they were both upset.

"Taligi just reminded me," Vai said, "that we must provide a ceremonial breakfast for Lotofaga and Salani this morning. That is part of the celebration I almost forgot. I just bought one hundred loaves of bread down the road but that's not nearly enough. I'm driving to Apia now for two hundred more. Your job is the jam, so get going."

I staggered out of bed and out into the night, wondering where one finds jam in a tropical forest before dawn. A papaya tree suddenly loomed before me. Papayas grew everywhere, planted by the birds in our new clearings. I picked a bushel and carried them home.

Dawn was just breaking and relatives were beginning to stir. I set four of them to peeling papaya and built a fire under two great iron pots. Vai arrived with a truckload of bread and drove on down to the villages. In an hour he was back.

"Hurry up," he called. "They won't eat it without jam."

I swung the steaming kettles on the pickup. Ten minutes later village ladies were jamming mountains of bread.

"Excellent," exclaimed a chief's wife, licking the knife, "is it peaches?"

The saofa'i was successful. The sixteenth Fuima and second Amitu was properly installed.

"Where is the food from the other Amitu?" I asked Vai, prepared to sympathize with the other faletua.

"Those two suckling pigs over there," Vai pointed out.

3 з3 зя33 3

"What!" I exclaimed. "Doesn't she understand what is expected? Cows, barrels of beef, and all that."

"There you are, thinking like a Westerner again," snorted Vai. "Can't you stop being materialistic? It's the spirit that counts." I wished he had explained that before.

Apa was right. We spent our last cent on that saofa'i but we gained about four hundred followers eager to call upon our chiefly leadership in solving their problems.

One of their most urgent problems was transportation. A week after the saofa'i twelve portly ladies swept up our driveway and adjusted themselves comfortably on the floor of the boys' fale. Vai was out in the plantation, so when I had mustered enough courage, I went over alone and sat down with them. We smiled and nodded at each other for a few minutes. When it became apparent that I didn't know the customary form of greeting, the wife of a talking chief made a welcome speech for me. They were, it began to dawn on me, the Salani village organization for the wives of chiefs come to pay the new chief's wife a ceremonial call. In consternation, I thought of the "visitation" inspections and fines. I excused myself and rushed off to find Vai.

"What shall I do with them?" I asked anxiously. "Do they want to count my sheets?"

"Don't worry," Vai said. "First give them tobacco, then food. And for goodness' sake, *smile*."

I discovered a bundle of native tobacco left by one of Taligi's talking chiefs. My visitors accepted it graciously, rolled it in dried banana leaves, and were soon puffing on large, luxurious cigars. After a friendly supper they settled down for the night.

Two days later they finally communicated the purpose of their visit. An annual meeting of church women was being held in Apia and they needed transportation.

Vasiliu

. "That's just a holdup," I stormed to Vai. "You can't take a day off for that and who will pay for the gas?"

"Do you want them to stay indefinitely?" he asked simply.

Prod as we might we could not get them all into the pickup. We sent the remainder by bus, and I waved them a cheerful farewell.

About a week later the same twelve wound up the driveway again and settled down familiarly in the boys' fale.

I did not greet them with a smile. I ran to Vai instead.

"If you take them anywhere again," I stormed, "I'm going to quit being your faletua."

"When," he said with a patient sigh, "will you learn to handle Samoans? Why aren't you over there welcoming them?"

He went over to the fale and gave the ladies a smile and a handshake all around. After a short welcoming speech he went straight to the point. Could he help them in any way?

Yes, he could. They had to go to the Women's Committee meeting in Apia and needed transportation.

"Just step in the pickup, ladies," he gestured politely. "We will go immediately."

I glared at him while the ladies prodded themselves in. Vai was examining the back tire. Suddenly there was a sharp hissing of air.

"A terrible thing has just happened, ladies," Vai said, straightening up and dropping the valve cap into his pocket. "The tire is flat and I have no spare."

They unpacked themselves with difficulty and studied the offending part.

"What a shame," said a portly matron. "Perhaps we were too heavy for it." And they filed off down the road.

Vai gave me a wink. "It's easy if you know how," he said.

CHAPTER THIRTEEN

Matatufu

Soon thereafter Vai was called upon to arrange Salani's trip to Tutuila. Pago village had invited them, and of course appropriate gifts had to be exchanged. Shortly after its return, Salani issued a similar invitation to Pago.

"Vai," I said tossing him our checkbook, "one more Salani feast and we've had it. You simply cannot be both a good matai and a solvent farmer. It takes too much time and money. Why don't you make your fortune first? Then you might be able to support them in the style to which they think their ancestors were accustomed."

Vai was in distress. Somehow, something was wrong. Samoan custom and commercial farming just did not seem to mix despite the brilliant reasoning of our thesis. Sadly Vai withdrew from the life of Salani.

We no longer appeared at church where contributions were announced in a loud voice to an attentive congregation. What we could have contributed after we had paid our boys would have embarrassed our relatives. Other matai, unharassed by payrolls and capital investments, gladly contributed their entire family income. They wouldn't understand our parsimony.

Vai no longer sat in fono meetings with the other matai. Their young men would go on fishing or planting in their leisurely manner no matter how long the meeting. But our plantation had to be supervised every minute. We had shipping deadlines to meet. Time was important.

When visiting parties turned in the drive, we hid in the forest. I couldn't face the implications. If I admired another lady's sleeping mat she always gave it to me with a smile. But when she in turn admired my radio—I just couldn't bring myself to the proper Samoan response. Usually our visitors requested several hundred pounds of taro to meet an impending feast. We could have asked the same from them. The trouble was that we had it and they didn't. I had mortgaged my life's savings and my father's to raise it. I couldn't just give it away.

I retired from the fa'aSamoa with a sigh of relief—but not Vai. He was miserable. He felt lonely away from the buzz of the fono and the clamor of the relatives.

"I just don't feel like a Samoan, anymore," he sighed as he moped around the house. "What's the use of building a good plantation, anyway, if I can't use it to impress the fono and feed my relatives."

I was about to point out that the plantation might prove useful in paying our debts and sending the children to college, but I stopped. . . .

It occurred to me that mine were Western, not Samoan, reasons.

For several weeks Vai lay miserably on the living-room couch. He had lost interest in everything. Then one evening he suddenly sat up. The twinkle was back.

"I've got it!" he called, slapping his leg. "Why didn't I think of it before? Those village meetings are all right, they are just on the wrong track that's all. They spend all their time thinking about how to give away what they haven't got. If they spent half their time thinking how to produce something they would have something to give. Look at the land and labor lying around. Furthermore, if they raised something themselves they wouldn't have to bum it from us all the time."

"A noble thought," I agreed, relieved to find him alive again. "What are you going to do?"

"A producer's co-op," he said. "We were wrong about the co-op store and credit union. They don't produce anything. What we need is a co-op to raise and market taro!"

"Hope springs eternal," I said, "but remember Salani will want a founding feast. And you know who will provide the taro and tuna."

"Who said anything about Salani?" retorted Vai, "I'm too closely related to that place. I'm thinking of the little village of Matatufu halfway between Salani and Lotofaga. In Matatufu I would have the prestige of a visiting chief without the obligations. I won't have to give them anything because I am not related to them. I'm starting a producers' co-op there tomorrow."

Thereafter Lafulemu saw very little of Vai. But when we did see him he was happy and busy. He soon had the village thoroughly aroused. After a thousand years of leisurely consumption, Matatufu was suddenly infused with a desire to produce. The village council decided that each matai should plant one thousand taro tops a week for the producer's co-op. Every Saturday plots would be inspected. Anyone planting 999 or less would incur a fine of four pounds, to be used towards the founding feast.

I thought the fine was exorbitant, especially since I was the first one who had to pay it. Ula couldn't count to one thousand. But the fine did cause a land rush. People from Matatufu started to settle all around us along the road.

I awoke one morning to find a series of coconuts planted down the middle of our driveway. Since this constituted a claim, I reported it to Vai. He had some difficulty dislodging this eager producer.

"I am going to plant as close to you as possible," the young man insisted. "I want to be near the future."

Vai assured him that the future was just as bright one hundred yards north.

Neither Lotofaga nor Salani put up the slightest objection to Matatufu settling the land they had just been disputing. Lotofaga was deeply involved in preparing a dance for the United Nations Visiting Mission. Salani was collecting for its return engagement with Pago. For reasons I understood better later, they were delighted with Matatufu's new co-op.

Co-op plantations were weeded regularly, inspired by fines which no one could possibly afford to pay. Even Mother Nature supported the co-op. The taro worm scarcely raised its head that year. Rain was plentiful. As the great bulbs developed, the Department of Agriculture sent word of an untouched market for taro among Samoans in New Zealand. An experimental shipment of fifty cases grossed almost £250, an incredible price.

"Matatufu is about to become the wealthiest village in Samoa," Vai said proudly as he arranged for a further shipment of two hundred cases.

But he spoke too soon. Next day Lotofaga village made an official visit to Matatufu, bringing all its talking chiefs along. This great honor required that Matatufu present the guests a great feast with plenty, of course, for them to take home. The co-op felt the blow.

I had never heard a Samoan host complain before. But along with its new plantations Matatufu had apparently acquired a new sense of possession. At a hastily summoned meeting the chiefs asked Vai for help. It seemed that both Lotofaga and Salani were having a serious shortage of food. They had done almost no planting during their months of dancing practice for the United Nations and visitations to Pago. Now it was telling. They were both planning a series of visits to Matatufu.

"They have been counting on us all along," fumed a Matatufu chief. "That's why they never objected to our clearing their land."

Visitors arrived in force. Every matai had relatives from Salani and Lotofaga.

"The only thing we can do is to declare this taro taboo," Vai said finally.

"But you can only declare it taboo for some purpose like a church or a school," objected the chiefs. "Otherwise it would make us look selfish."

"We have got a purpose," replied Vai. "Every penny from the producers' co-op is going to build a co-op store."

They hastily agreed. The taro was declared taboo even to themselves. It was being saved to build a store. Salani and Lotofaga were understandably offended.

"Matatufu," they huffed, "has repudiated the Samoan way of life."

"They're right," I laughed, "Matatufu is beginning to think like businessmen."

But the taboo did not solve the basic problem. Lotofaga and Salani really were hungry. Breadfruit would not be ripe for six weeks. Villagers scoured the forests for wild yams and edible roots. Before long they began raiding Matatufu's plantations at night.

In old Samoa, stealing was a meaningless concept. One can't have stealing if ownership is not felt. Besides there was never much to take. But nine months of co-operative effort had made Matatufu a "have" village and had changed its outlook.

"What we need is a policeman," the village council decided. The nearest police station was in Apia. Remember-

ing our tuna, Vai had some misgivings about this, but he went to town with their request.

"I have never had a request of this type before," the superintendent of police told Vai. "We couldn't possibly begin to police plantations. But since a producers' co-op is unique too, I'll lend you a man as an experiment."

The Apia policeman lasted only one night. He didn't "steal" anything but he arrived complete with relatives. Of course, it was only polite to give them baskets to take home.

The village council met again.

"Why don't we select our own policeman?" suggested someone.

"No good," another pointed out, "anyone we could select would have relatives."

Eventually they hit on a solution. They would all become policemen in rotating patrols of five so that they could also watch each other. They equipped themselves with shotguns.

Instead of introducing peace and prosperity as we had intended, we had changed the little village of Matatufu into an armed camp. For a month or so there was great tension along the coast. By no means all of the protected taro made its way to New Zealand, but there was enough for several large shipments. With a sigh of relief Matatufu packed its last case and prepared to make peace with its neighbors. I expect it had to prepare an apology feast for its offense. No one proposed to plant again.

The taro had brought well over the five hundred pounds necessary to start the Matatufu co-op store. At a meeting to discuss this event, however, Vai discovered that the matai were already deeply in debt for most of it. With an eye on their burgeoning plantations, private merchants had been generous with credit. Matatufu had managed to eat most of its cake before it was baked.

With special assessments Vai managed to salvage £150, enough to build a one-room store but not to stock it.

"My feeling is that we should put up the building anyway," he told me. "Otherwise the £150 will vanish too."

The prospect of a building revived the flagging spirits of the Matatufu co-op. But where were they to put it? The village already had one little store at the far western end. Obviously the co-op should serve the center and east. The co-op President, Tau, offered to remove his own fale to make room for the store, providing his own family could live in the store, of course. The law, however, required a regular lease. So Tau offered a piece of his plantation land just at the eastern edge of the village. He was delighted to find that leases paid rent and immediately put this discovery to practical use. As the co-op was erected, another little store took shape on the same plot, not a hundred yards away. Tau had rented that location to the store from the western end. But no one was in the least dismayed at having the two stores side by side. It was beginning to look like a shopping center.

The co-op looked something like a very small motel— one room, one door, one window. But it was brightly painted. Co-op members were so proud of it that they took turns living there. But they could not get over their disappointment at having no stock on the shelves.

Vai proposed another round of taro production. Tau proposed hiring an uncle who had once been a "businessman." This uncle had contact with an Apia store which would be glad to stock the co-op. A democratic vote was taken on the two proposals. It was perfectly clear that all but ourselves preferred borrowing to production. Reluctantly Vai resigned from the co-op store.

The next time we visited Matatufu the co-op was in full swing under the management of Tau's uncle. The store at the other end of the lot was also in business, managed by Tau himself. Relations between the two stores were excellent.

We did not see Tau again for four months. Then he appeared at the plantation one evening accompanied by his wife and children—all were in tears. They had, they sobbed, encountered two catastrophes. Vai was the only one to whom they could turn for help.

First, as president of the Matatufu co-op, Tau wanted a loan of twenty-five pounds to restock the store. The shelves were bare again.

His second problem was that as manager of the Apia branch store in Matatufu, he had had an even more distressing experience. Not only had he been fired, but he had been taken to court by the parent firm. Only an immediate loan of fifty pounds could save him from imprisonment.

"Let's help him," Vai pleaded with me. "He was my right hand man in the co-op."

"What happened?" I demanded sternly.

Apparently Tau's intake in cash had not corresponded with his outgo of stock by a considerable amount.

"Why not?" I asked.

"I don't know," he sobbed. "I didn't take anything."

"You didn't by any chance sell on credit?" I probed.

"Of course," he said. "I had to do business."

"Well, give the court a list of the creditors," I said. "That should clear you."

"I did," he wailed, "but they weren't satisfied. Something didn't add up."

"That's odd," I said. "Are you sure you wrote all the names down?"

"Oh, yes," Tau assured me. "I can't write but my son can. Every weekend when he came home from school I told him what everyone had taken during the week. I'm sure he wrote it down. He's in high school, you know."

CHAPTER FOURTEEN

Beachcombers and Archaeologists

My mother was concerned. During our second year of residence on the plantation she wrote, "Don't you get lonesome out there in the forest, twenty-eight miles from the nearest town? Don't you wish you could speak English with someone?"

All I could reply was, "Hardly." Lafulemu was rapidly becoming a tourist and academic attraction.

It may have been due to Aggie Grey, whose kindly interest had followed us ever since that midnight when we moved into the basement of her little hotel. Now, when guests wanted to get out of Apia and "see Samoan life" she often suggested they visit us.

We were delighted. We took them down to see the crack and served them coffee in our living room.

"So this is a Samoan fale," they often exclaimed as they examined the louvered walls and wooden water tank designed by my father. "It is so pleasant to meet a real Samoan family."

Vai winked at me and whispered, "I guess you must be making progress as a chief's wife, honey."

Often our guests were very helpful. One Hawaiian couple

was searching for an albino coconut. We weren't much help but they later sent us seeds for solo papaya and Hawaiian passion fruit. Another couple sent us vegetable seeds from Australia.

One evening an Italian count dropped in, bearded, barefooted, and with a pack on his back. He found touring the world a rest from Italian politics. He was traversing Samoa on foot searching for that tantalizing, legendary lady with the golden hair. I wasn't much help on her, either.

We discovered Samoan art with a reporter from *Life*, and Samoan sex with a psychiatrist from Philadelphia. I was introduced to parapsychology by a couple from Australia who were stalking Samoan ghosts. With the aid of number cards flashed behind a screen, they discovered that Samoans were just about as psychic as anyone else.

By far the most well known of our visitors, however, was the "lady beachcomber." No one was exactly sure where she originated, but she was moving across the Pacific rapidly at government expense. The governor of Tahiti had shipped her to Pago. The governor of American Samoa had sent her on to Upolu.

We first caught sight of her up in a tree at a church dedication at Satalo. No one could possibly have missed her. She was dressed in a very tight black skirt and a very brief white halter and was gesticulating wildly and calling, "Can anybody here speak English?"

Vai stepped to her assistance with his customary chivalry. She leaped at him from the tree with an agility remarkable in a lady of her age. Seizing his arm she whispered tensely, "I'm so glad you have come. I was desperate. My interpreter just ran off—ran off, mind you, and left me here alone with all these primitive people."

Vai, surprised, looked around at his friends—the medical practitioner, the agriculture agent, the village teacher, and the district judge. They all spoke good English. But these "primitive" gentlemen were all coughing into their hand-kerchiefs.

For the rest of the day the lady beachcomber kept Vai in sight. He seemed to restore her self-confidence. When she was not darting up trees, she was asking questions and interrupting ceremonies to take countless snapshots.

"I am a photographic journalist," she confided to me, whipping out a notebook. "Now tell me again, slowly, what is this ceremony about?"

As we walked home along the coast that evening Vai said, "I really felt sorry for that lady. Everyone was laughing at her. I invited her over to Lafulemu for the weekend. Perhaps you could hint to her that halters are not in style with us."

Next day in Apia he mentioned our prospective guest to Aggie Grey.

"So she's got around as far as you," said Aggie with a hearty laugh. "I've tossed her out of my house twice already. She thought that journalists should get free board and room. Why, bless you, all she's got in this world is that camera. From me she went to Gardiner's place. When she told them their children were too noisy they suggested she see more of village life and shipped her to the south coast. Vai, my boy, just don't let her settle down."

The High Commissioner knew her too. "Well, I'm relieved she's turned up at last," he told Vai. "She came to my office several days ago and ordered a government car complete with chauffeur and interpreter. I sent an interpreter, mostly to keep track of her, but in a few hours he was back. He felt people were laughing at him. On these islands we have to be careful of people who want to settle down on Samoan hospitality. If you have any trouble with her let me know."

Our guest arrived on Saturday morning and we took her

for a picnic. She was in a pathetic mood and soon told her troubles to Vai.

"Nobody here seems to like me," she said sadly. "I wish I knew why."

"In Samoan custom," Vai said kindly, "we lean over backwards not to appear to be demanding."

I looked at him in astonishment.

But she took his advice to heart. "You are so kind to take me in," she said turning to me. "Isn't there something I could buy for your new home?"

"Oh, no indeed," I said hastily. "I don't need a thing. If you want to snap a picture of my children, I would love to send one to my mother, however."

On Sunday we took her to Salani. When the midday meal was over the chiefs leaned back against their posts and looked at her for a long time.

"How old are you?" one of them asked abruptly.

"Oh, about forty," she said, blushing.

"Are you married?" asked another.

"Well, I was married once," she stammered.

"What happened to your husband?"

"He died."

"Would you like to marry again?"

"Why yes," she answered vaguely.

"How about that chief over there?" he pointed across the room.

We all looked. There sat Leasu. He really looked darling. He couldn't have been more than five feet tall or more than twenty years old. His face was round and boyish with enormous black eyes. Today a big red hibiscus nodded over his ear. At this sudden attention he jumped to his feet with embarrassment and ran out to hide behind a coconut tree.

"Why yes," said the lady, brightening. "Does he really want to get married?"

"He's yours," said the chief, "but it must be a real Samoan

wedding, of course. As representative of your family Vai must provide fifteen fine mats, five tuna, and twenty bags of taro. We will set the wedding for Wednesday."

"This is going too far," I whispered to Vai. "I think they mean it." But Vai didn't hear. He was rocking with laughter.

On Monday I woke our guest early.

"I'm sorry to disturb you," I said, "but the bus goes by here early and I don't want you to miss your appointments in Apia. I know how busy you journalists are."

She sat up with a hurt expression. "But I thought you wanted me to take some pictures of the children for your mother!"

So I had.

She was a very careful photographer. She spent the morning finding a perfect background, but by that time the sun's rays had passed it. The picture had to wait until Tuesday morning.

We spent the evening discussing art photography. She had been having her trials in Apia. No studio there took proper care in developing her pictures, she told me. Artistic work like hers demanded particular skill. She had her own special developer in Australia, but for a year now he had been stealing her films. She was penniless. She was particularly puzzled about what to do with the pictures of my children.

"I would like to see them developed in America," she said, "to bring out their true quality. But of course I have no dollars."

"Well, since one is for my mother anyway," I said, "let's send the roll to her. She would be glad to develop them, and send back the others."

"A fine idea," she agreed. "Give me her address and I'll post the film in Apia tomorrow."

Next day we took four pictures of the children. Tuesday evening I had a serious talk with Vai.

"She must leave by the first bus tomorrow," I said. "We can't take any chances with that wedding."

"Just leave it to me," said Vai.

I heard him thanking her for spending so much time on our pictures. He agreed to waken her early in time for the bus.

Next morning we both went to rouse her. She had vanished! The bus came and went. Vai and I felt worried and guilty by turns. Perhaps we had hurt her feelings. But an hour later she ran gaily into the kitchen in her bathing suit.

"My," she called, "the water is wonderful this morning. I couldn't tear myself away."

I was speechless, but not Vai.

"We have just had bad news," he said hastily. "My father is ill. We are leaving for Manono immediately. Could we drop you in Apia on the way?"

"I'm sorry to hear that," she replied earnestly. "Isn't there something I could do to help you? I could stay and watch the plantation for you while you are gone."

"That's very kind of you," said Vai, "but I wouldn't think of letting you take the risk. You know these 'primitive people.' It isn't at all safe for a girl to stay alone, especially if she is about to be married."

We deposited the lady beachcomber in front of the Apia town clock.

"Sorry we can't drive you home," said Vai, "but we must hurry. You can get a bus from here to just about anywhere." We waved a friendly farewell.

A fortnight later the High Commissioner put her on a boat for Fiji. The end had come when she joined the United Nations inspection trip to Savaii and wanted to ride in the official car.

But that was not the last we heard of the lady beachcomber. A month later I got a box full of pictures of Australia and Tahiti, and a puzzled note from my mother.

"I can't figure out why you wanted 120 shots developed," she wrote, "when only four of them were of the children. It cost me $8."

It was fortunate for the lady beachcomber that I did not have her forwarding address. I shoved her pictures into my desk and forgot about them.

But she didn't. Six months later I received a letter from Australia:

"I can't understand why you haven't forwarded my valuable pictures of the islands."

I tossed her box into the mail without comment. Two months later I received a letter from South Africa.

"I am notifying the police that two of the valuable pictures I entrusted to you for development are missing."

Some of our most interesting guests were not tourists but visiting experts. There was the New Zealand engineer, for example, who stopped in for a day. He had been sent to investigate the *Joyita* mystery. The *Joyita* was a private motor launch which had come to Samoa to fish. It had offered to lift some passengers and officials to the Tokelaus and then disappeared completely. Some said the captain was a fugitive from justice and had taken them all to an uncharted island. Others were convinced that a flying saucer had snapped them up for exhibition on Mars. After a month the waterlogged hull was found near Fiji, the life rafts and passengers missing. The engineer had been sent to examine the hull in Fiji and check on its condition when leaving Apia. So far he had noted that she was traveling with a broken radio transmitter, and without an auxiliary pump.

Two geologists came by to look at our crack.

"Eleven lava flows on top of each other here," they told us, "coming from somewhere west of the Mafa Pass."

A geographer asked us to help him locate a missing waterfall. But our favorite guest was Charlie, the soil specialist.

"Feel the forest floor with your bare feet," he told us. "It is cool and damp even on the hottest days and thick with fallen leaves. As you change over to commercial crops always keep it that way. If it is exposed even a day to the blazing sun or a tropical rain, it can be ruined. This is no country for a plow. Samoans have the right idea; they cut a little patch here, another there, and then move on. They put the weeds right down on the ground again. They raise taro, bananas, cocoa, and coconuts all mixed up together. It may look like a jungle but those things shade each other like the original forest. It is the new, not the old, agriculture that threatens the land."

His mind was an adventure in itself. He had been to Antarctica to study the rocks. In the jungles of northern Brazil he had met the daughter of a vanishing Indian tribe. He said he was returning shortly to marry her and build a plantation where white men had never been before.

Charlie did not propose to study Samoa by car. Instead he tramped for days through the mountaintops where even Samoans rarely go.

One evening he dropped in from the forest, his face ruddy from a day of tramping. "What's the Samoan story about these forests?" he suddenly asked Vai. "Did anyone ever live up here before?"

"I have heard about Vaigafa village up near the Mafa in Tongan times," said Vai. "But that's all."

"Then I think several chapters in Samoan history are missing," said Charlie seriously. "When I walk through these forests I climb over hundreds of mounds of rock. They don't look natural to me."

"I know what you mean," said Vai. "Samoans call them *tias*. They say the old Samoans built them as pigeon blinds. They set up their traps on them."

"That's a heck of a lot of work for a pigeon," said Charlie, "and if there had been that many blinds you wouldn't find a single pigeon in Samoa today. I'm wondering if they weren't fale floors from old villages. When I go back to New Zealand I'm going to talk an archaeologist into coming up here."

A few weeks later I was standing on a knoll under a huge kava tree, scolding the boys. "You can't plant taro like that," I said, pulling up a loose top. "You know very well the hole should be at least a foot deep. And you must twist your planting stick so there is a ridge of dirt around the hole. Like this—"

I seized the iron-pointed stick and rammed it through the leaves as hard as I could. Crack! It hit a rock so hard that I nearly fell over. The boys laughed. I tried again and again. When I didn't hit a rock I hit an empty crack. I finally threw the stick down in disgust and marched home to tell Vai to supervise his own boys.

"Maybe you hit one of Charlie's rock piles," Vai suggested.

"With a big tree growing out of the top of it?" I asked sarcastically.

But I did ask the boys if they had ever noticed a *tia* in our forests. They shrugged indifferently. The subject did not interest them.

But it continued to intrigue Charlie and ourselves.

A year later when visiting at Aggie's we were introduced to three visiting archaeologists from New Zealand. Goldman, the tall one, was a professor. Billy, the bearded one, was his assistant, and Sally was an American Fulbright scholar. Anthropologists are a dime a dozen in the islands but archaeologists were something new.

"I'm glad you came down," I said politely, "Charlie says we have some amazing things in our forests."

"Actually these wet tropical islands aren't too fruitful for archaeologists," the professor told me. "Samoans made almost all their things from leaves and bark which disintegrated immediately. All we can hope for is a few axe heads and rock floors. It isn't like Egypt or Mesa Verde where the food is still on the table, you know. But what did Charlie say he saw?"

"Tias," I said, "everywhere."

"Maybe you could show us one."

That was embarrassing. I wasn't sure I had ever seen one myself, except perhaps the knoll where I couldn't plant taro. But it would be fun to have Sally as a visitor.

"Sure," I said. "Come out to Lafulemu and stay with us this weekend."

On Saturday I showed the archaeologists my knoll, trying to hide the fact that it was covered with large trees.

"Let's pull up some of these vines," Billy suggested.

With the help of the boys we uncovered a section. No wonder I had planting trouble. It was solid rock.

"This is very interesting," the professor mused. "Look here, these rocks are fitted."

Sure enough, a well-built wall was emerging.

"But no one would build his house around these trees," I protested.

"You forget," Sally explained, "these trees can't be more than several hundred years old. This floor might be a thousand."

They had seen plenty of tias before. But this one, they claimed, was unusual. Instead of steps like most fales, this one had six ramps running up to the main platform, giving it somewhat the shape of a star.

"I have seen only one other like it," said the professor,

"the one they call the 'star house' on the top of Manono island."

Our schoolboys watched our excitement with tolerant smiles. "So what? It's just another pigeon blind," one said.

"I don't think so," the professor replied, "because it seems to be part of a village."

We looked around us in amazement. Now that our eyes were opened we could see tias everywhere among the trees. A strange feeling swept over me. Instead of being a pioneer in a virgin rain forest I was merely a latecomer to a culture which had flourished while my ancestors were immersed in the Dark Ages. These forests were once full of people.

In the afternoon Sally discovered a pasture where Noti's cows had thoughtfully consumed the vines. Suddenly we found we were looking at acres and acres of fale floors, roads, ditches, walls, and round pits where we had seen only pasture before. It was astonishing.

"This wasn't a village," said Billy. "It was a city."

"You know what we should look for?" suggested Vai, "Vaigafa village up near the Mafa. There are lots of stories about it so it must have been more recent than these forgotten tias." He took us up to the site by car.

Every Samoan along the road knew where Vaigafa had stood. They even remembered the location of the separate houses. A chief volunteered to take us to the very spot on the bank of a little creek. Once there, we looked around us in surprise. No tias, no ditches, no holes, not even a stone. The forest looked as if it had been empty since the creation.

"Where did you say this village was?" the professor asked again.

"Right here," said the chief positively. "The houses were placed in a circle on this open piece. The women washed on that flat rock over there in the river."

"Then they must have taken their floors with them,"

Billy smiled. "I bet that was the real Vaigafa down in Noti's pasture."

Vai motioned me urgently aside.

"Don't breathe a word to that chief of what the archaeologists are saying," he warned me. "Vaigafa village is the basis of claims to this mountaintop."

It still is.

That evening we lounged around the living room, listening to Sally strum old American ballads on her guitar. "Not too different, really, from the nightly compositions of our own boys," I thought.

"What I need now," the professor was saying, "is to get inside a tia. I wish I had one that was cut cleanly in two."

"Oh, no," groaned Billy, "it's hard enough to get the vines off."

A few weeks later they both had their wish. In the process of roadbuilding, a bulldozer had cut squarely through a large mound at Vailele, one of the government plantations. The professor and Billy pounced on it. It was an archaeologist's dream.

Sally invited me out to see it. They had cut one side into neat steps and were excavating these in one foot square blocks with a spoon and brush.

"See these four layers of large rocks," the professor pointed them out on the side of the cut. "They each represent a separate fale floor, built one on top of the other. Look at the two lower ones. They each have a layer of black above them. It is carbon, which means they were probably oven pits. The layers of dirt in between means the site may have been used for a plantation as it is now. But there is little doubt that four houses at least, have been erected on this mound."

Then he showed us his major discovery. I was slightly disappointed. It looked like a dirty little piece of flat stone bent slightly at the edges, but he handled it like a baby.

"What is it?" I asked.

"Pottery," he said almost reverently.

"What's so wonderful about pottery?" I asked Sally later on. "Every archaeologist digs that up."

"Not in Samoa," she told me. "It has always been assumed that Samoans were not pottery-making people. Besides, did you notice that it was blackened? That is carbon from a cooking fire. The professor is taking it to New Zealand to have it carbon dated. Then we will know exactly when that pot was on the fire."

It was several years before I heard the conclusion. That fire had burned 1950 years ago! It was the earliest verified date in all Polynesia. The archaeological world apparently had the same reaction to that pot that I had to my tia. It threw Polynesian history into a new perspective. People must have been living in Samoa five hundred years before anyone had figured, and maybe long before that. It was probably no new arrival who had cooked food in such a well-turned pot in such a well-built fale.

The true saga of the islands of the sea and how they were peopled, has yet to be told. But the story may well cover a thousand years more than we had thought.

CHAPTER FIFTEEN

All in the Family

As in Tutuila, the size of our family circle was not limited to the possibilities of biological reproduction. Only this time we tried daughters instead of sons. When Ata left with Mo'e she apparently forgot one of her offspring, a bright little girl of eight who had never seen a day of schooling in her life. Lisa promptly came up and joined our household. Since Ata left no forwarding address there was not much I could do but take her in.

Lisa's past should have given her a psychosis. She was the first of Ata's children by a Satalo chief. Like many Samoan attachments, the arrangement was never formalized, but the chief apparently thought highly of Ata. He killed a man in an argument over her and was sentenced to eight years in prison. While he was away she had four more children by another husband. Lisa was brought up by her grandfather. In recent years Ata had undertaken a third and legal marriage with Mo'e, but, scarcely out of adolescence himself, he did not care for children. Lisa was the only child Ata brought with her to Lafulemu, and Mo'e beat Lisa as often as he did her mother.

"If you don't stop that," I scolded him once, much distressed, "I'll take her away from you."

"You can have her," he retorted. Perhaps that's why he left without her.

Strangely enough, Lisa was as happy and well adjusted a child as Dr. Spock could have wished. She spoke cheerfully of her mother and Mo'e, and was not the least disconcerted by their sudden disappearance.

"That's not so surprising," Vai told me. "In our big families children are not attached to one mother. They are attached to many. I had four adopted mothers myself. I seldom lived with my own. It is a whole community of relatives, not one person, that gives our children security. Desertion and adoption don't bother them a bit."

At first Lisa was a typical little Samoan girl. She took charge of dishwashing and toddlers as a matter of course. She never spoke to me unless spoken to, and then only in the most respectful terms. This did not imply that she was always obedient. It merely meant that instead of presenting a flat "no" like my daughter, she said "yes" with a charming smile and proceeded to do exactly as she pleased. I was somewhat confused by this, especially because she was always prepared with the most ingenious excuses. Soon, however, I began to realize that Samoan children and American children were more alike than appeared at first glance. Samoan children developed different tactics, that's all, because of the more authoritarian relationship between parents and children.

Lisa had almost no cultural lag. She began sitting at a table, eating with a knife and fork, sleeping in a bed, and speaking in English as if it were second nature. She was enthusiastic about everything, especially Santa Claus, a gentleman whose existence she had never dreamed of. Her amazement made Christmas a special treat for all of us.

But something soon began to bother me about Lisa. I couldn't put my finger on it at first. When she asked me for a good-night kiss it took me by surprise. When she hid my shoe and laughed like a pixie, I couldn't believe it. When she roared for second helpings at dessert and tore across the living room in front of guests, I was shocked.

But why should I be? She was acting exactly like my own children. Suddenly I laughed to myself. What seemed normal in my offspring seemed incongruous in her only because I had subconsciously thought of her as a Samoan. She just wasn't acting Samoan anymore.

A few months later we went to visit the pastor's home at Lotofaga. Prominent members of the congregation were seated in a circle on the mats.

"Lisa," called the pastor, about to send her for a hymn book.

"What do you want?" she called gaily, spinning around a post with one hand.

Every Samoan present was stupified. Any other child would have bowed quietly and knelt at the pastor's side for instructions. Her brazenness was unthinkable.

There was a long silence. Everyone stared at Lisa. Then their eyes shifted and they stared at me. What had I done to her?

The seriousness of my crime dawned suddenly upon me. In my heedless hospitality I had been preparing Lisa for a culture which she would never see. Without a thought I was making her a shocking misfit among her own people. I lowered my eyes in humiliation.

"We must send her back to her grandfather immediately," said Vai on the way home.

I was sorry to lose Lisa with her restless energy. I think she was sorry to leave us though she went as blithely as she had come. Could her grandfather repair the damage I had done?

Two weeks later we visited him. We had just finished a tranquil meal in his fale when I spied a familiar face in the cooking house behind.

"Lisa," I called.

She bowed quietly in the back of the house and knelt at my side for instructions.

Mata was another temporary member of the family. She was a large girl of about twenty-five, with a dull, square face. Once she had been a school teacher but for reasons undisclosed she had been unemployed for several years. Vai's uncle sent her to us so that she could recuperate from the flu. Somehow she was related to us.

She spent most of her time sitting on the doorstep in the sun, staring vacantly at a tree. Since she had been ill I didn't press her. She had sudden spurts of interest, however. I came back from the plantation one day to find her and the current housegirl unpacking and examining all my trunks.

"What do you think you're doing?" I asked angrily.

"Your clothes need airing," she replied blandly.

One Friday morning a few weeks later she suddenly announced that she was leaving.

Being in no mood to protest I simply said, "Well, toss your bags in the car. I'm driving in to Apia in about an hour."

"No," she said flatly, "I'm taking the bus," and she padded off down the road. I shrugged my shoulders, wondering idly if she were eloping. That might brighten her up a bit, I thought.

That afternoon I was discussing stew meat with the butcher in Apia when the bank teller tapped my shoulder.

"Could you tell me please," he asked somewhat urgently, "did you sign this check?"

The check was for thirty pounds, made out to cash. It was my name all right, but not my writing.

"No, I didn't," I said. "I doubt if I have that much money in the whole world."

"Oh dear," he said. "I cashed it. The check was from your book, you know."

I checked the number with my book. He was right. It had been torn from the last page.

"Do you have any idea who might have done it?" he inquired.

I thought carefully. The checkbook hadn't been out of my purse in Apia, so it must have been someone at Lafulemu. Not the housegirl, she was still at home. It must have been . . .

"Yes," I sighed, "I have an idea."

"Well, would you please go with this policeman and make an identification."

The policeman and I did not have far to go. We met Mata at the next corner. She gave me a vague nod as the policeman escorted her to the station.

Mata was the culprit. They found some new filmy underwear and twenty-seven pounds in her purse. She admitted readily enough that it had been by virtue of my checkbook.

Next day her matai, Vai's uncle, visited me.

"Just tell the police she's your relative and ask them to release her," he said, as if it were a matter of course.

"I couldn't do that even if I wanted to," I pointed out. "It is the bank that is prosecuting her, not me."

He couldn't see why that should make any difference and went off to talk with Vai.

"You've got to try to get her out," Vai told me later. "She's our relative, remember."

"What difference does that make?" I snapped. "If she feels so close to us why did she steal our money?"

"But you don't understand," Vai insisted, "she's my uncle's stepdaughter. The family will be furious with us."

"Why aren't they furious with Mata, instead?" I asked.

"Mata didn't break up the family, and that's just what you're doing," Vai groaned.

He was right. Family relations became very tense. Cousins refused to recognize us on the street and the normal channels of supply and demand inside the family were disrupted.

"Oh, bother," I finally decided. "Who am I to break up a happy tribe?" I went to see the Superintendent of Police.

"Don't tell me why you've come," he said, throwing up his hands. "You want Mata. Don't you know she's our best case? For years now we have been trying to bring forgeries to trial. It's a real problem in the bank. But we can't get people to prosecute. They're usually related and afraid they will break up their families. I was so happy when I heard you were an American. Now, what's the matter with you? Haven't you got any guts?"

"Well, let's put it this way," I said. "As the wife of a chief I am pressing no charges. Mata is my husband's uncle's stepdaughter and for goodness' sake, release her so the family can quiet down. As a product of Western culture, however, I am all behind you. Pull her in before any more of my cousins get the same idea."

"As far as I am concerned you are an American," he laughed, "but I will tell the relatives that you tried."

The day of Mata's trial arrived.

"We must go by all means," said Vai, "to show the family we are standing by them."

The courthouse porch was covered with relatives, many of whom glared at me with outright hostility. Vai's uncle bustled over and pulled him aside.

"I've solved the problem," he said. "This is what we are going to do. Mata will plead guilty. The judge will give her the alternative of jail or fine. I'll choose the fine and you pay it."

"Well, I'll be darned," I burst out, "who . . . ?" Vai gave me a swift kick.

"That's a good idea," he nodded hastily to the matai and pushed me through the door.

Mata sat up in front of the court wearing a shining orange and black sateen dress which did everything possible for her girth. She was enjoying the day immensely. Never had she felt her relatives so solidly behind her. When the judge asked her if she were guilty as accused, she nodded vigorously and smiled at her admirers.

"Then you have clearly violated a position of trust," said the New Zealand judge in a matter-of-fact tone. "Your hostess trusted you; the bank trusted you; and you failed them both. This sort of thing must be stopped in Samoa. I hereby sentence you to one year in jail with no alternative fine."

A great wail went up from the relatives. Her matai sprang up waving his arms.

"Clear the court," pounded the judge, and a policeman pushed us all out.

Lamentation continued in the street. A woman rushed up hissing something at me in Samoan. I smiled politely, having no idea what she had said. But my sister-in-law who was standing beside me leapt at her like a cat. Soon they were tearing each other's hair and a crowd gathered around us.

"Police!" I called, running back towards the courthouse. A policeman appeared and pulled the ladies out of each other's hair.

"What in the world did that lady say?" I asked my panting sister-in-law.

"She called you a pig," flamed my defender.

Vai pulled me hastily into a car and slammed the door.

"Now," he said, "you see what comes of your American ideas?"

"All right, all right," I sobbed, "I'll apologize to her matai."

A few days later I saw Vai's uncle.

"I'm sorry about Mata," I said, "that jail sentence was tough luck."

"Not at all, not at all," he said pleasantly. "I'm glad to have her out of the house for a while. Never knew what I would be missing next while she was around. The food up there is fine, she says, and they are teaching her to sew. She's having a wonderful time. Why don't you take her a cake next Sunday?"

A year later I saw Mata on the street. She had on a new and becoming dress. She smiled and gave me a little wave.

"Good news," called Vai, bringing in the mail one day. "Nu'u, my sister Fetu's husband, is going to the States. Lafi is paying his fare and your sister is putting up the bond for him."

"That's nice," I said. "What is he going to do there?"

"He will study for the ministry. High school in four years, college in four years, and two years of divinity school. In ten years he'll be the first B.D. in our whole family of ministers. It will make my father very happy."

"I guess the Methodist Mission will be happy too," I said.

"No," Vai said frowning, "the missionaries are all against it. Sometimes I wonder if they want Samoans to be educated. They tried to stop him by saying he had a wife and five children to support."

"Well, doesn't he?" I asked. "Who *will* take care of Fetu and the children while he is gone?"

"We will, of course," said Vai, as if I had asked a silly question. "They'll be moving out here next week."

"Look, Vai," I pleaded, "as soon as our plantation breaks even, OK. But right now we are still living on my father's savings and we can hardly squeak by."

"That's enough," said Vai firmly. "Your ideas broke me off from my village and my uncle, but from my parents and my sisters—never. They're coming."

Fetu was well provided with household equipment. It came by long-boat to Salani and five pickup loads to Lafulemu. We established the family in the boys' fale.

"Perhaps," I schemed with myself, "I can make her self-supporting as a foreman or something."

Fetu had a face like a madonna, though the rest of her was somewhat expansive. She was a gentle and restful soul, for years the mistress of her husband's little Methodist church in Sataua. Every girl in the parish had sat at her knee.

Her five children were just like her. Placid, with moonlike faces and fragile little limbs. They were much less trouble than my own.

That was fortunate because they came over to my house for their meals and stayed all day. I watched the budget with consternation. Instead of a fortnight, one case of milk lasted only a week. The meat bill doubled and so did eggs and rice. None of them had eaten like that before and they loved every mouthful. I was glad to see them put weight on their slim little frames. But I was also worried.

"I'm sorry, Vai," I said, "I love them all, but I just can't make ends meet. We're not eating Samoan food, you know. Milk and eggs are Western food. They come from New Zealand and they cost a lot."

"Just be patient," Vai said. "By next month Fetu will be running this plantation for us."

At the end of the next month she was by no means running the plantation. My housegirl was doing her cleaning and laundry.

"This is a hard period of adjustment for Fetu," Vai explained to me. "Remember she is a pastor's wife and has been waited on hand and foot by the village girls. This is very new to her. Wait a while longer and you will see."

But next month she was still adjusting.

"Vai," I said, "I need my housegirl back. You will have

to tell Fetu that she must wash her own children's clothes. She has been in siesta since eight o'clock this morning and hasn't rolled over yet."

Vai agreed to speak to her.

"We must be easy on her," he told me when he returned. "I have just learned that she is three months pregnant."

A few days later we had cinnamon rolls for supper. Fetu was especially fond of these. We sat around in a mellow mood after the children had gone to bed.

"Fetu," said Vai finally, "I have been thinking of our father. He and mother are getting old now. The village sends them food, and gives them a house, but they need someone to direct the girls and to see that everything is dignified as it should be in a pastor's house. I would send Fay except that she knows nothing about such things. But you are a pastor's wife—you could do it well."

She nodded. "He does need me," she said simply, "I must go."

I felt ashamed. I never did dare thank Vai because I was never sure whether it was me or Fetu or his father whom he meant to benefit.

I just looked at him with admiration. "You will make a great matai someday," I thought to myself. "You seem to have a genius for human relationships."

CHAPTER SIXTEEN

New Generation

Samoa, says the Stace Report, has the fastest-growing population in the world. I have never doubted it for a moment. Vai's father's fourteen children had already presented him with fifty-three grandchildren by the time I arrived, and that was only a beginning, since six of his sons were still in school. What I hadn't counted on was adding so substantially to family tradition myself.

Our fourth baby was born shortly after a hasty ride over the Mafa Pass and into Apia. Far from succumbing to her rigorous environment, Riki was the largest and lustiest of all. She was also the hungriest. I had gathered from watching the fat, happy heirs of Salani that demand feeding probably produced pleasant, easygoing personalities. They were hugged and cuddled and fed whenever their little hearts or tummies felt the slightest twinge, and they responded to life with the greatest equanimity. Not Riki. The more I obliged the more she demanded. Every hour or two, Lama, our newest housegirl, beat on a large iron frying pan with a hammer to let me know my daughter was hungry again. Across the river the boys looked up from their work and set off to find me, out in the forest, down

in the gorge, or tracking runaway pigs. The whole plantation was upset. Here was a baby who, unlike most Samoan
children, was heard but not seen.

The three older children, Gloria, Buddy, and Chippy,
developed the opposite means of commanding attention. It
was their absence, rather than their presence, which
brought the rest of us to our feet. One morning I sent them
out to play on their favorite "Jungle Jim," an enormous tree
which had been felled in the front yard, and which now
lay devoid of leaves, branches reaching forlornly into the
air like the bones of an ancient whale. It looked grim to
me but it provided endless adventures and bruises to
three-, four-, and five-year-olds. Half an hour later it occurred to me that the yard was unusually quiet. I called to
the children but got no reply. Setting the baby down, I went
out to look behind the trunk, into the holes, and up in the
branches. The tree was deserted. I called into the bananas
on every side, but the only response was the rustling of the
trade wind in the leaves. I hastened down the path, expecting to find three bobbing heads around every turn. Five
minutes later I could hear the roaring of the river as it
dropped fifty feet into that awful crack. My heart suddenly
seemed to stop beating. Could the children possibly have
gone this far? A few minutes later I slid down the banks
of the ravine. Suddenly I stopped and my hands froze
around the root of a tree. Just below me, in the middle of
the log bridge, sixty-five feet above that roaring torrent,
stood Buddy. He was calmly watching the chaos below him.
My first impulse was to scream. My second was not to
breathe, lest he turn around and tumble in. I crouched
there for an eternity, not daring to move my eyes for a
moment as if my gaze alone could tie him to the spot.
Presently he looked up and sauntered on across the log to
the other side. When his feet touched solid rock, I suddenly felt limp.

"Buddy," I called in a weak voice, "sit right down where you are."

He did not seem at all surprised to hear me. He waved gaily and obeyed. When he was firmly settled, I called, "Now tell me, Buddy, where are Gloria and Chippy?"

"Don' know," he responded cheerfully, tossing a stone into the crack. "They was right behin' me a minute ago."

Something seemed to buzz inside my head. This was a nightmare—and now the moment to wake up. But I didn't wake up. I crawled down the bank and screamed, "Gloria! Chippy!" into the thundering crack until my breaking voice bounced weakly off the walls. But I knew it was no use. No one could possibly hold on against that pounding black water, or climb back up those dripping walls. They must have been swept inevitably on and over the 120-foot falls into the great gorge below. I rolled over on my back and closed my eyes, letting wave after wave of agony sweep over me.

I have no idea how long I lay there. A group of our boys returning from work on the other side found Buddy still sitting beside the crack. One of them hoisted him onto his shoulder and with much laughter brought him back across the log. They found me lying prostrate on the other side. I couldn't explain. I just pointed into the crack and they gathered the rest from my expression. Without a word, most of them fanned out along the river and through the forest, walking downstream. One of them took Buddy back to the house and said he would return with a rope. Another went to look for Vai. I just lay there, too sick to move.

About twenty minutes later I heard a shout ringing through the forest. It was answered by another, and I sat up. A few minutes later four of the boys scrambled down the bank and helped me up. They had found five-year-old Gloria and three-year-old Chippy, hand in hand, walking down the main road towards Lotofaga. Gloria explained that she had decided to go back to the road since the log looked too difficult for Chippy.

"Seems Gloria looks after him better than you do," Vai said coldly, but I didn't mind. I was just too relieved to have four little sleepyheads to tuck in bed that night.

Once in a sociology class I had heard about "marginal men," pitiful people who wander in a never-never land between two cultures, unable to identify with either one or the other. I was not troubled with this particular problem myself. It was becoming all too clear that I could never be more nor less than an ordinary middle-class American. But sometimes I wondered about my children.

After my experience with Lisa, the problem took on more urgent form. It was easy to see that Lisa should be brought up in a Samoan way. She would undoubtedly spend the rest of her life on this island. But with my own children, who could say? I certainly didn't want to predetermine the issue for them.

After some thought I decided that the trouble with "marginal men" was that they looked at themselves as "half-castes." They didn't quite know how to behave in either culture. I determined to raise my brood as "double castes," fluent in both languages and equally able to handle a kava cup or a coffee cup. The difficulty was that I wasn't too sure about the fa'aSamoa myself. I purchased a book on Samoan custom, and read carefully the chapter on the kava ceremony. When entering the fale, I learned, newcomers shake hands around the circle and seat themselves quickly at their proper posts. After the kava has been squeezed, an announcer calls the names of the recipients in order of status. The bearer raises the cup to his forehead and carries it to the chief mentioned. If he is not sure which chief is which, the proper recipient indicates his position by clapping his hands.

Obviously the kava ceremony lent itself to role playing. I

acted it out several times with the children, assuring them they would surprise their father with their grasp of Samoan custom.

When Vai next went down to Salani I suggested he take Buddy with him. "I have given him some role-playing lessons," I said, "but he needs firsthand experience. I think you will be surprised how much he knows."

Vai was surprised all right. Instead of crouching outside with the other children, Buddy followed his father right into the fale and shook hands around the circle. The old chiefs didn't know what to do. It was the first time in their experience that they had been formally presented with the hand of a four-year-old. Protocol just didn't extend to such a situation. Out of deference to Vai they tried to pretend Buddy wasn't really there. Several times Vai tried to shove him over the side and into the flower garden with a surreptitious prod of the knee, but Buddy only looked hurt.

When the chiefs sat down at their ceremonial posts around the fale, Vai tried to solve the problem by handing his son over to a girl outside. A few moments later Buddy was back, sitting solemnly a few posts down. By this time the ceremony had begun and Vai didn't dare get up. Nobody moved.

Buddy watched the distribution of the kava with polite interest. Once, when the bearer seemed in doubt, he clapped his hands twice. The bearer twirled around in his direction, and then turned red with embarrassment. There was a ghost of laughter from outside the house, but the chiefs proceeded with imperturbable dignity. Vai was frozen to the spot with mortification.

While the announcer was saying the closing words it became clear to Buddy that he was not going to be served. He rose to his feet, crossed the floor, and scooped up a tiny cupful from the sacred kava bowl for himself. Raising it to his forehead he started back to his place. The announcer's voice stopped in mid-air. Forgetting his manners, Vai jumped up, scooped his son under his arm, and ran out of the village.

As soon as they reached home I could see that Buddy's firsthand experience with Samoan custom had been a traumatic one, at least for his father.

"Promise me," said Vai with tight lips, "that you will never, never again give our children any lessons on Samoan custom. Especially no role playing. You just teach them how to behave in Washington, D.C. I'll send them to my sister for anything else they need to know."

It was amazing, however, how much they picked up without any guidance from me. Try as I might, there was always a certain formality between myself and the boys working on the plantation. I was the one who gave orders, and we never got far beyond that. They were quite different with my children, however. I have never seen adolescent boys have such a good time with little children. They romped and roughhoused and sang and told amazing stories, until Gloria and Buddy and Chippy were bug-eyed with admiration and refused to listen any longer to "The Little Red Hen." The language problem never occurred to any of them. They just seemed to be born understanding Samoan stories. I looked longingly at their linguistic development. It seemed so easy compared to my unrewarding struggles with Churchward's grammar.

Soon the children were well beyond my level. On more than one occasion I discovered what a guest was saying by oblique assistance from the little characters playing at my feet.

"*Fa'amolemole lava sina vai aisa,*" requested a guest.

"Now run along and get it for him, dear," I would say to Gloria, wondering what in the world "*vai aisa*" could be. I realized that this method of covering my ignorance had its risks, and felt quite relieved when Gloria returned with a glass of ice water instead of Vai's best shoes. But that moment of tension was always helpful in establishing a new word in my vocabulary.

Chippy's first word was in Samoan, and I was so delighted I forgot to inquire what it meant. It sounded somewhat like a little cowboy on a roundup, "Eye kai." In any case it always aroused such bursts of laughter and applause from the boys that it was soon firmly established in Chippy's vocabulary. He used it upon every occasion, and always at the top of his lungs.

When Vai's father next visited us I explained proudly that Chippy was learning Samoan. I knew that would please him. He nodded his head approvingly.

"I hope you have been teaching him from the Methodist catechism," he said.

To cover up my shortcomings I called Chippy from his blocks.

"Say something to Grandpa," I suggested.

"*Eye kai*," shouted Chippy obediently.

The color drained from Grandpa's face. His eyes seemed to double in size and blackness, as he slowly turned and stared at me. All I could do was smile and nod vigorously. But the old man didn't say a word. He pulled himself to his feet and went to look for Vai.

"Have you been teaching Chippy Samoan?" Vai asked me sternly that evening.

"How could I?" I replied, thinking the answer was obvious.

"Where *is* he learning it, then?" Vai asked.

"It just seems to come to him naturally," I pointed out.

"Well, don't tell my father that," Vai said hastily. "Do you know what Chippy said to him this afternoon?"

It suddenly occurred to me that I had not asked Chippy for a translation. "No," I faltered.

Vai enlightened me forthwith. I groaned.

"As a result I had to promise my father that I would teach Chippy from the Methodist catechism," Vai concluded, "and he intends to examine him on it before the whole congregation on White Sunday."

"Well, you will have to take full responsibility for that experience," I said flatly. Vai agreed.

Vai took the assignment to heart. White Sunday was six weeks away but he rehearsed the children every evening. They learned a Samoan song which they sang together in a piercing treble. Then the two older children recited a long passage which had something to do with obeying one's parents. Finally Chippy was drilled on the Methodist catechism. Six weeks revealed that he was not capable of progressing beyond the first question, but he learned that thoroughly.

> Question: *O ai na faia oe?*
>   (Who created you?)
>
> Answer: *O le Atua.*
>   (God.)

All over Samoa the next generation was being similarly rehearsed by eager pastors and fond parents, for White Sunday in Samoa is a most important church occasion. It is like Thanksgiving and Christmas rolled into one and placed in the middle of October. The idea for White Sunday must be credited to the London Missionary Society. It was to be a sort of Children's Sunday. In a country where half the population is under twenty, the idea was a staggering success. Other denominations soon had to conform. Today White Sunday is the occasion when the children take over the church service with countless recitations and playlets. It is a day when relatives from all over the island gather for feasts after church, around kegs of beef, tins of biscuits, huge roast pigs, and gallons of ice cream. On this one day the parents serve the children and let them eat first rather than last. White Sunday, not Christmas, is when the children get their presents, usually candy and white suits and dresses for the coming year. So many bed sheets are lost the week before White Sunday, the hospital of American Samoa has threatened to dye its linen blue.

My contribution to the festivities was three white dresses for our girls and daughters, and three fitted lavalavas with pockets for Vai and our sons.

"I never thought I would be making skirts for my menfolk," I pointed out, but secretly I was quite satisfied. They are so much easier than pants.

On Saturday I baked twelve cakes while Vai conducted a dress rehearsal. The children were in fine form.

Early Sunday morning we packed the cakes, several hundred pounds of taro, twenty pumpkins, and four starched children into the pickup. We unpacked them sixty miles later, dusty and limp, in Salamumu.

The three-hour morning service was drawing to a close when we arrived, but that was not a matter of great concern. Less than half the village children had had time to recite, so there would be another three-hour service in the afternoon.

At least we were in time for the feast. Relatives had collected from everywhere and children were legion. For this one day in the year they were very much in evidence and making the most of it. Instead of crouching quietly around the edge of the house, as usual, they crowded gaily inside and sat down at the chiefs' posts. The adults served. This reversal caused great hilarity on both sides. The climax of the feast was "ice cream," a lukewarm mixture of sugar and evaporated milk served in glasses. Things ended with a candy toss which swept Grandfather right off his feet in a swirl of shrieking grandchildren. White Sunday was well designed for Samoa.

At three o'clock the service began again. The church was

packed and sweltering. The white paper flowers on the headbands of the little girls drooped and fell into their eyes. Some of the recitations were stylized playlets. The children stood in two stiff lines and shook their fists at each other, declaiming at the top of their lungs. These renditions looked as if they might have derived from the Orient. Most of the pieces were sing-song passages not one whit different in tone, inflection, or content from the one on obedience which my own children were so ably prepared to give. And over and over again,

"*O ai na faia oe?*"
(Who created you?)

"*O le Atua.*"
(God.)

But such is the love of a mother that I sat with anticipation for two hours until my own should come to glory.

At last Vai's father called them to the front. There was an expectant hush and a craning of necks, as if here were something a little different. I could only hope that it wouldn't be. Gloria and Buddy sang and recited exactly like all the children who had preceded them. If I had closed my eyes I couldn't have told they were my own.

Finally Grandfather bent over and put his hand on Chippy's curly head as if to prevent any further recurrence of his past experience with this little man.

"*O- ai- na- faia- oe?*"
(Who created you?)

he asked slowly and distinctly, as if to prevent any possible misunderstanding.

"*O'u MATUA.*"
(My parents.)

shouted Chippy, smiling triumphantly at his grandfather.

CHAPTER SEVENTEEN

Alone

While we were building our plantation, Samoa was progressing along the road to independence. The prospect of a Polynesian island with a Polynesian culture under a Polynesian government thrilled Vai.

"The Hawaiians, the Tahitians, the Maoris all gave in," he said, "but not we Samoans. Our culture is still Polynesian. We may be poor but we are proud of the way we live. It is all our own."

"But even Samoa must enter the twentieth century," I hazarded.

"Who says she can't," he laughed. "We won't have to rely on tapa cloth and stone adzes to keep us Samoan if we have our independence. Does your mother dress like a Pilgrim in order to preserve the American way of life? That's not the way a culture is preserved. A healthy culture satisfies the problems its people have. It changes to keep up with them. The real question is only, who does the changing? If the West provides the goals and the answers for us we will no longer be Samoan. We would be just one of their 'backward areas.' But if we decide our own goals and provide our own answers who cares if we are different, who cares if we are poor; we will be living the way we want, in a way we understand, and we certainly won't have to worry about remaining Samoan."

The Constitutional Convention of 1954 selected two of the four paramount chiefs as Heads of State. These two gentlemen felt just as Vai did. They wanted independence and without a lot of hesitation. The way to learn is by doing and Samoa was quite prepared to start immediately.

Tamasese, one Head of State, and Vai discussed these things at length.

"One of the keys to self-government," Tam said to Vai, "is the Public Service Commissioner's job. After all, he is the man who hires, fires, and controls the public servants. We have never had a Samoan in that job. We have had some well-intentioned New Zealanders but something in their mentality leads them to believe they have discovered the *only* way of doing things and that it will take fifteen years of training to convince a Samoan to do likewise. They have been preparing us for self-government since 1914 and they still can't believe we are ready. Furthermore it is hard for outsiders to understand Samoans. They tend to overestimate our yesmen and discourage our original thinkers. They certainly are a pushover for our more devious characters. In my opinion, despite their degrees, they haven't got the right background for the job and they don't take time to provide themselves with it. They can't even speak the language. It takes a Samoan to understand a Samoan and handle him effectively."

"I know," smiled Vai. "My wife has similar handicaps."

"A really good Public Service Commissioner should have an overseas degree and a Samoan heart," continued Tam, "but he must also have guts. When a New Zealander talks about 'training Samoans to take over,' he means everyone's job but his own, you know. A lot of them wouldn't feel too secure with a Commissioner who really meant to replace them with local people. They're only human, after all. A Samoan commissioner would also have to face our own people, and hold his own. We're not immune to jealousy, you know.

"Vai, you're the only Samoan with educational qualifications they can't dispute. You could never earn what you could on a plantation, but it would be a big step towards independence. It will take time, but the assistant commissioner's job is open now. May I suggest your name?"

"Oh, no!" I cried, when Vai told me Tam's proposal. "Every cent of my savings and my father's is in this plantation—and two years of our lives. Our first crops are just coming in. What did you tell him?"

"That it was up to my wife," said Vai simply.

That was a decision to wrestle with and I spent the night at it. Was our income important to Vai? The subject scarcely ever crossed his mind. Was farming really his first love? He spent most of his time at meetings in Salani and Matatufu. Was he mechanically minded? He was the fellow who forgot to screw the nuts back on when he changed a tire.

I had to face facts. Vai's heart was in politics—not plantations; in people—not in banana cases. Above all it was Samoan.

"Go ahead," I told him in the morning with a wave of resignation. "This plantation would probably do better under an American anyway."

"That's my girl," he said, giving me a hug, and ran to catch the bus.

I stood there alone looking at the plantation across the river. The pointed spears of the banana stalks were just beginning to shoot up among the fringed leaves. As far as I could see, forest had given way to fruit. To me it was a thrilling sight. My capitalist background stirred within me. Plantations were certainly as important as politics in the attainment of self-government. I would make mine a model of productive efficiency. Instead of carrying Salani on my back like Vai, I would give that village something to catch up with. Who cared whether my plantation was run in a Samoan, American, or Chinese way? What really mattered was—did it raise bananas?

What we need first, I said to myself, is some long-range planning. No more of this living from day to day. I sat down at my desk and produced a notebook.

First, I would survey the plantation with a compass, laying it out in one-acre blocks indicated by coconuts. That would tell us not only how many acres we had planted, but could help us forecast production and assign work efficiently.

Second, no more pay by the day. I couldn't possibly follow twenty weeders and sprayers around to see how often they went to sleep. I would assign them definite spots and pay them by the acre. Then they could sleep at their own expense.

Third, I would post a daily work schedule and announce it with a bell:

6 A.M.	Reveille and breakfast
7 –11 A.M.	Morning work
11– 2 P.M.	Lunch and rest
2 – 5 P.M.	Afternoon work
5 – 7 P.M.	Bath and supper
7 – 9 P.M.	Prayers and school
9 P.M.	Lights out

Seven hours of work wouldn't hurt them and with that schedule tacked on the post they might think twice about singing all night. As a further thought, I appended a list of rules of conduct on the plantation and set myself a daily tour of inspection.

Fourth, I would introduce laborsaving devices. One obvious improvement would be to clear paths along the acre lines so the boys wouldn't stagger over the trunks and through the weeds and vines with heavy loads of bananas. It was silly that no one had thought of that before. We would also set up a decent packing station on assembly-line principles. And perhaps—happy dream!—a cable to sling bananas over that awesome crack.

I snapped my notebook shut efficiently. We Americans really did have a good idea or two. Now it was only a question of putting them into effect.

My knowledge of surveying was derived solely from a Girl Scout badge called "map-making." For a month I criss-crossed the forest with a compass and line and two boys to clear the way and cut pegs. I loved every day of it. The boys introduced me to drinking vines. Slashed with a knife, this wonderful weed dropped half a cup of water, cool and pungent as the forest, into a thirsty mouth. I also had a personal encounter with *salako*, a tree that has the properties of poison ivy magnified by ten. We tracked wild pigs, followed the purr of the Samoan dove, examined trees where bats hung motionless all day, and played a game called "rooster" with the curled ends of gigantic ferns. To these boys every tree, every root, every leaf, had its own particular use. I was the only stranger in this forest.

We discovered that we had already cleared 112 acres in a rather irregular shape, and planted 85 of them. We also discovered that Pu'a, a matai from Salani who had signed our land agreement, had removed a section of our fence and was cutting long thin lines through our part of the forest in every direction. I was furious. If he could play that game, so could I.

I hired a crew from Vailoa to cut a line a quarter of a mile long and a few feet wide, crossing the ends of all of his lines. That should stop him. The ring of their axes brought Pu'a with his relatives on the run. Soon both sides were cutting furiously. Pu'a and I paced our respective clearings, glaring at each other through the trees, and giving orders like embattled generals. The court finally stopped this war by enjoining us both.

"Now see what you have done," lamented Vai.

"What *I* have done!" I exclaimed. "Pu'a started cutting on the land he signed over to us. Did *he* bother to get an agreement with the chiefs the way we did?"

"Well, I'll just have to go and call off that court case," said Vai.

"Call it off!" I cried. "But a court case is just what we want. We have Pu'a's signature that we can clear that land. Now we will see how good those agreements are and settle this crosscutting racket once and for all. I think we will win."

"Of course we will win," Vai agreed patiently, "but that's hardly the point. Use your head. If we win Pu'a and his relatives will be furious. How much taro do you think you would get off your land then? What are you going to do, live over there in a tent to watch it? Don't expect the other Salani chiefs to back you up, either. They don't think much of airing village differences in public courts."

"Don't tell me you're going to give in after all this!" I said, aghast.

"Oh, no," said Vai, "but we will settle it in Samoan fashion." I had my doubts.

Vai had three meetings with the Salani chiefs. Much was said. Much was consumed. Nothing was decided. Then we all forgot about it. Neither Pu'a nor myself went near our battle lines. The bush took over again.

Three years later Vai chanced to meet Pu'a. Five minutes of pleasant conversation resulted in a line satisfactory to both sides, since by then both of us had lost interest in the affair.

Meanwhile, after surveying, I spent most of my time inspecting. It was no mean task to locate boys who were weeding in that nodding sea of sun-flecked leaf and vine. With bodies the color of earth and sunshine, a ragged cloth at the waist, and garlands of fragrant leaves around their necks, they could disappear while one looked at them. One evening I almost sat down on an octogenarian who was crouching in the waving taro rubbing up a fire for his cigar.

The fact that no one cared to be inspected added to my difficulty. One afternoon I completely lost Ualese. For an hour I called and searched. No weeding, no Ualese. On my way home I glanced down into the gorge below the falls. Two hundred feet straight below me at the base of the thundering waterfall, a body lay inert on the rocks. This was almost as bad as the children. Ualese must have slipped from the log bridge and been swept over the falls! I raced home and came back with a rope and two boys. Nothing but belaying could get a rescuer down that cliff. And what good would it do? Ualese must be dead.

The three of us lay down flat on the edge and peeked into the abyss. Before our very eyes the body moved, sat up, stretched leisurely, and lit a cigarette. Ualese had found a place free from inspections! But it must have taken him all day to get down there.

"That settles it," I told Vai that evening. "I can't follow these boys around all day to see if they are working. I can't even find them most of the time. I am going to introduce my second innovation, work by the piece instead of work by the day. Then they can rest on their own time without having to jump over the cliff."

When Falefa village arrived next Monday, I informed them that workers would be paid sixpence for every banana planted: twopence for the hole, twopence for carrying the banana stump, and twopence for planting it. We all agreed that this was a just arrangement. I showed them where to start work, and took a well-earned rest from inspections.

Three days later Falefa reported that they had completed the four acres assigned. I went with them to check it. It was considerably more work than I had supposed, counting up hundreds of little banana stumps hidden behind logs and under fallen branches. We never did agree on a figure. I agreed to their count, however, and cheerfully enough. I had about halved the price and time of planting bananas.

Several weeks later I proudly demonstrated the area to Vai.

"That's fine," he nodded approvingly. Then his eyes narrowed. "Do you notice something funny?" he asked, puzzled. "A lot of these banana stumps haven't sprouted yet. Only about one in three." Sure enough, next to every sprouting stump were two rotting ones in regular order.

Vai considered the problem a moment. He leaned over and pulled up an unsprouted stump. There were no roots on the bottom at all, just a clean knife cut. We pulled up others. They were the same.

Vai suddenly roared with laughter. "Those boys are one up on your piecework game," he said. "You see what they have done? They cut the banana trunks into three pieces and planted all three. It saved them a lot of carrying and looked the same to you. But of course only the piece with the root on it is growing."

I couldn't share his amusement. "Don't look so angry, honey," Vai said. "I'll tell the mayor of Falefa on these crafty characters tomorrow. He will have them make amends."

A few days later I drove down to Falefa to let the mayor know when the group should come back to replant its rootless bananas. As I entered the village I noticed that a feast was in preparation. My erstwhile workers waved at me gaily as they ran by with loaded shoulder sticks.

"Welcome!" one called.

I stopped him. "What's going on?" I asked.

"Oh, don't you know?" he said surprised. "We are preparing a five-pig feast for the mayor. It's our fine for being tricky with your bananas. I'm sure he would be glad to have you attend."

One of my most trying problems was banana spraying. Samoa is blessed with a tiny moth whose delicate scale on maturing bananas makes them unsuitable for packing. If the pod of the banana is opened and the immature hands sprayed with DDT within a day after the stem has bent down, this scab can be eliminated. Every day I had four boys hunt and spray newly turned pods. Even at best they scarcely found half of them; the rest were a complete loss. I couldn't say much, however, since I could never find the pods either. Since I certainly couldn't follow all four sprayers at once to see if they kept going, someone in the Department of Agriculture suggested that I have the boys cut off the tip of each pod they sprayed and hand these in at night as an indication that they had at least made the rounds. I added a piecework touch and offered them twopence for each tip brought me at the end of the day.

The effect was miraculous. Pod tips jumped from twenty a day to over one hundred. What a fortune Lafulemu would make when this great crop ripened in three months! I entered the number of tips on a chart and applied for banana cases accordingly.

But the great day never seemed to arrive. Three months later when one hundred bunches should have matured every day we were still packing only one hundred bunches a fortnight. I ran over my figures again. I had paid for

2,587 tips and had harvested only 223 bunches therefrom. Something was definitely wrong!

I thought about the problem for a while. Then sadly I got into the pickup and drove up and down the road. My worst fears were confirmed. The tip of every pod from Lotofaga to Falefa was missing. I had been purchasing them from everyone in the district!

After evening prayers I had a serious talk with the boys.

"Yes, we did import tips a month or so ago," they admitted, "but we will never do it again."

I soon discovered why. They had hit upon a more rewarding method. Several mornings later I came upon our four sprayers seated in a circle deep in the plantation. Before them was a great stock of banana pods. As I watched from behind a banana leaf I saw them busily slice the pods crosswise like a loaf of bread. Amid pleasant chatter they peeled each slice down like an onion to the center. At the center of each slice was a little tip just like the one at the bottom of the pod. Out of a single pod they could thus make six or eight tips without spraying a thing! Small wonder they didn't send to Lotofaga for them.

Regretfully I abandoned piecework payment for banana spraying.

Instead I proceeded to my third reform, a daily work schedule. Appreciating the general lack of experience in working to a bell I broached the issue democratically. I asked the boys themselves to suggest a schedule, providing it included only three meals and at least seven working hours. They soon produced a satisfactory arrangement which I drew up artistically and posted for their benefit on a post of the house.

The only problem now was the bell. Ships have bells, but I can say with authority that none of them were purchased from stores in Apia. They don't sell any. Time was too pressing to hollow out a large log and make a Samoan drum. Someone suggested a compressed air cylinder. But the ones left by the American Army had long since been turned into church bells. I finally hung up a crowbar. This had a beautiful tone but two defects. The first was that it required someone to ring it. The obvious person for that job was myself since I was the only one interested in schedules, but I had one serious disqualification. I couldn't bear to get up at six o'clock in the morning. The second defect was that its tone must have closely resembled some Samoan birdcall. I have never heard this bird, but the boys did. Regularly every morning and afternoon, they tramped back from the plantation one hour early insisting they had heard the bell.

Working on a schedule brought up another even more serious problem. I had always counted on the boys for odd jobs like chopping wood for the outdoor oven, washing pots, and catching midnight crayfish. They did these jobs cheerfully enough, just as they always had at home, until I posted that schedule. Then it took them exactly twenty-four hours to develop the concept of overtime. Every move became a collective bargaining and accounting operation, involving calculations of time, price, and multiples of one and a half. The price of crayfish went up from nothing to five shillings a dozen. Schedules were just not worth the inflationary rise in the cost of living. I gradually ceased to enforce them.

Maybe we didn't see eye to eye on piecework and time schedules, but there was one subject upon which the boys and I could certainly agree—laborsaving devices.

I started to clear paths following my survey lines. Once I had cleaned these, the banana sprayers could take a regular route rather than stumble aimlessly here and there through the weeds. Their daily trips would keep the paths clean and usable as boundary lines for piecework. It couldn't fail.

The boys liked the idea too. They chopped roots and stumps and pulled vines and rocks out of the way at the rate of three shillings a side. Our plantation must have looked like a gigantic checkerboard from the air.

But only for two weeks. After that the weeds obliterated our paths completely, lush, green, and impenetrable as ever. Only two muddy tracks remained clear, meandering here and there over logs and around stumps in a roughly diagonal direction across the plantation.

"How did this happen?" I asked the sprayers. "Why didn't you use the paths we prepared? Just walking on them every day would keep them open."

"Those square paths are no laborsaving device," they insisted. "They take too much walking."

By far the most sophisticated laborsaving device, however, was our cable. What hours of unnecessary toil it would save if we could pack the banana cases on the plantation side of the river, sling them lightly across the crack, and deposit them directly on the back of a truck for shipment to Apia. Perhaps I could ride the cable myself and avoid that sickening feeling every time I crossed the log.

I have never seen an engineer on the job, but I'm sure we approached the cable problem in the proper manner. First, I surveyed the terrain. Plenty of good, stout hardwoods grew on both banks above the crack. It should be no trick at all to run a cable between two of them. I selected two likely prospects, measured the distance, and drew a diagram.

I took this picture to Apia and purchased the necessary supplies: a ½-inch cable ninety feet long, two heavy pulleys, and a roll of one-inch rope. This sling would surely convince both Salani and Vai of the efficacy of American ideas. I would have it in full operation by the weekend.

All that was needed, obviously, was to attach the cable to the trees. I called the boys to help me. Our first discovery was that cables cannot be tied in knots. A close study of the Sears, Roebuck catalogue revealed that one should use clips. Our next discovery was that even a small cable is unbelievably heavy. We attached it to a tree and rolled it across the crack. But we couldn't begin to pull it tight, even with the help of an expanding crowd of eager spectators. We couldn't even hold onto it. It kept whipping itself back into the crack in a most ferocious manner.

The problem rested there for a few days until a friendly New Zealand schoolteacher broke down on a motorcycle outside our door. We watched him repair his machine with some admiration, and invited him to look at our engineering problem.

"What you need here is a winch," he said.

When it became clear that none of us knew what a winch was, he offered to come out on Saturday and build it himself. We were very grateful.

Dick was as good as his word, but a winch was not an easy problem, we discovered. He sank two cement shafts into the ground with loops of iron embedded in them. Through these he laid a heavy log with holes bored in it.

"When the cement is dry," he said, "just attach the cable to this log, stick a crowbar into the hole and wind the cable onto the log. If you leave the crowbar in, it will snap back against the ground and keep the winch from unrolling. Simple as that!"

We waited impatiently until the cement had set. Then the whole neighborhood took a holiday to witness the birth of the machine age in the forests of Falealili. I acted as midwife, instructing the boys in the intricacies of winching.

We passed the cable through the notch of a tree and down to the log and fastened it with a clip. Dick was right. A boy with a crowbar at each end of the log could pull the cable tight as you please. The crowd cheered. But

I looked twice. The cable was running downhill. That would never do.

We detached everything. Our oldest boy climbed the farther tree like a monkey and reattached the cable about thirty feet higher up. We winched again. The cable stretched out straight and level. Everyone cheered again.

Now for the first ride. Everyone looked at me.

"Oh, no," I said hastily. "You need me on the ground for engineering advice in case anything goes wrong. But of course nothing will go wrong. Those cables never break. Now who is going first?"

Everyone looked at each other and then down to the crack where the black torrent thundered along only to plunge over the lip of the falls and into the gorge far below. There were no volunteers.

"Oh, come now," I encouraged. "This first trip is free. After this I'll probably charge for fares to Falealili."

No answer. I looked around desperately. There was Ula, our youngest boy and my best pupil.

"Come on, Ula," I called gaily, "if you go first, I'll give you my cowboy hat."

That hat was a great temptation to Ula, and no sacrifice to me. He always wore it anyway. It was an enormous sombrero from Mexico, and it made little Ula look like a mushroom on legs.

He got up slowly and walked over to the nearer tree. The crowd shouted with delight, so he couldn't change his mind. He climbed into an enormous packing box which we had fixed onto the traveler. The crowd cheered again. Falling into the spirit of the occasion he waved the sombrero and suddenly sailed off into space.

Ula was not very heavy, but perhaps the box was. The cable sagged alarmingly though the winch did not give an inch. Ula and the box rushed downhill and stopped suddenly—suspended right above the crack.

vasilio

For a long time we could see nothing in the box except the hat. Then slowly it rose and two enormous frightened eyes peered over the edge and down to the torrent a hundred feet below. Then both hat and eyes disappeared again.

"Pull him in!" I shouted to the boys. They shouldered the lead rope and swung the box a few feet uphill, but that was as far as they could get it. Others volunteered from the crowd. Everyone shouted advice. But the best they could do was to draw the box half way up the other side.

"Now don't panic," I told everyone, swallowing hard, "just pull him back over here where he came from."

The boys shifted back to my side and pulled again with exactly the same result.

"The winch," I said desperately. "Let's pull him in on the winch."

We all moved back to the winch with friendly assurances to Ula. Just in time, somebody pointed out that the cable was already on the winch, and attaching the rope would just unwind Ula into the crack.

We tried pulling again to keep Ula's spirits up, but it was no use. I was forced to my last resort.

"Let's wait until Vai comes home," I said.

For several hours we sat there in silence. The box swayed gently over the crack, but there was no sign of Ula, not even the hat.

At six o'clock Vai came striding down the bank. We all rushed to explain the difficulty. Vai was as bewildered as the rest of us, but he exuded confidence.

"Now two of you boys go up in the tree and try pulling from up there. Ula," he called, "wake up and help pull the box up along the cable with your hands."

The boys scrambled up the tree. But there was no response from the box.

"Do people really die of fright?" I wondered.

With the greatest effort, Vai and the boys got the box three quarters of the way up the other side. But they couldn't bring it an inch more. Just before dark, Ula's brother took the final step—or rather leap. Pushing himself off from the tree he swung down the cable by his hands and scrambled into Ula's box. Then with the help of the boys on the rope, he pulled Ula, the box, and himself up the cable to the tree. Ula was lowered together with his hat, pale but still alive. He wouldn't look at me.

"It's just a slight mechanical defect, really," I explained to Vai at supper. "We didn't tighten that cable quite enough."

"And if you did get it tight," he said, cracking a taro with his hands, "just how do you propose lifting the banana cases thirty feet up that tree to start them off. They don't climb as well as the boys, you know."

That was a point which hadn't occured to me.

Once I had exhausted my list of innovations, things moved on more placidly for the boys—but not for me. I seemed to live in a perennial state of tension with Samoan custom. There were packing days with 150 cases of bananas to be at the ship by 10 P.M., and everyone off at a wedding. There were paydays when no one could remember just who had planted what, or someone had weeded an unmeasurable arc instead of a square. There were arguments about who bought what at the store.

"Your wife is a very hard woman," they told Vai.

In November there was an incredible infestation of large green worms which ate our taro plants to the ground and left twenty-five acres as desolate as the Egyptian pestilence. And there were always the four rambunctious little Ala'i's to keep out of the crack. It seemed to be all work and no progress.

At the end of the year the Department of Agriculture sent us an astonishing bit of news, however. Lafulemu was the third largest banana producer on the island. That was the proudest day of my life.

CHAPTER EIGHTEEN

No Good-by

Taro did not have the conventional effect on me. It is supposed to be fattening, but the more I raised, and the more I ate, the thinner I got. Vai watched with some concern my slimming figure. Samoans like well-rounded, placid, obedient wives, adapted to a lifetime of pleasant conversation with an endless succession of visitors. Every day I was becoming less like the ideal version.

Finally, he said, "Honey, the time has come to hire a regular manager for Lafulemu. The children must begin school. That's your job. We can find someone else for the bananas."

The latter was an optimistic overstatement. Entrepreneurial ability is not one of the strong points of Samoan genius. We had plenty of applicants, each complete with a large staff of relatives. But invariably they assumed that plantations could be run from a sitting position, and that storekeeping was a good-will operation.

Finally my sister solved the problem. In New York City, she met a British colonial planter and his South African wife who had spent time in India and were interested in tropical plantations. We exchanged letters.

They were, they assured us, quite used to working with people of different cultures. We explained our situation as clearly as we could and apparently they liked it. A few months later George and Mabel landed in Samoa together with a generator, a theodolite, pith helmets, and two fat dachshunds.

We greeted all these improvements with open arms. That was just what Lafulemu needed, agricultural know-how with a tropical slant, and an improved breed of dog.

The dachshunds, we learned, were a very important part of their family. Each carried a passport with photo and paw print. The photos flattered them somewhat, I thought privately, or had they gained weight recently?

Mabel was enchanted with her first glimpse of Samoan villages, but apparently our plantation was a bit of a shock.

"She's just tired," George explained. "She'll recover in a few days."

Our children were beside themselves with delight at the dachshunds. At Mabel's request we banished all lesser forms of dog life from the plantation—and we had accumulated quite a variety. The dachshunds reigned supreme. They ate special dog meat from Apia, enjoyed daily beauty treatments, and aired themselves on a double harness every afternoon at three. Their presence gave the plantation an almost urbane atmosphere.

May seventh was the dachshunds' birthday. Mabel warned me of the impending event and made them a most exquisite birthday cake. She had purchased candles and ribbons for the occasion months before in India. To the utter delight of the children and the utter incredulity of every Samoan on the south coast, the dachshunds sat at the children's table licking the frosting while we all sang "Happy Birthday" to them.

Mabel was a magnificent cook. She could take all the bones out of a fish and put it together again with salad dressing and pimentos so that even its own mother would not recognize it. Her accomplishments would have looked well on the chef's table at the Astor. The boys took their cans of sardines and made stew for themselves over a fire in the back yard. But Vai and I benefited enormously under the new regime.

Cooking was a whole-day affair for Mabel, and I was glad of it, because she soon informed me that she hated agriculture. Apparently the deplorable situation in which she now found herself was due to a semantic difficulty over the word "plantation." In Africa, she told me, "plantation" meant a couple of thousand acres of well-pruned cocoa trees, a porticoed villa, and fifty black servants with white gloves. To call Lafulemu a plantation had been quite misleading.

The enormity of my error dawned upon me. Here I had lured this flower of the colonies ten thousand miles from home to a little cement platform in the middle of a newly cleared jungle.

Mabel disliked children as much as she adored dogs. Though she didn't mention it directly I suddenly became aware that my babies were wearing less than the conventional amount of clothing, and that they made an ungodly amount of noise.

"I knew another family once which had difficulty disciplining its young," she told me pointedly. "The boy turned out to be a thief and the girl a prostitute."

So that she should never discover the full extent of the children's primitive capacities, I banished them to the boys' fale during the day. Both the boys and the children enjoyed that.

One thing Mabel did enjoy was bridge. Vai played with her every evening after supper. Unfortunately I could never keep my eyes open long enough to join them. Mabel also liked entertaining. But entertaining at Lafulemu had never advanced beyond the picnic stage, and that was not what she had in mind. As often as we could, we sent her to our friends in Apia. She was a gorgeous sight stepping on the bus with a hobble skirt and two-inch heels. I often wondered what she looked like when she stepped off the bus after twenty-eight miles on a wooden bench sitting amid greasy baskets of roast pig, and innumerable bouncing babies.

George too had his problems. I had mentioned that we owned a pickup truck, a chain saw, a grindstone, and a set of carpenter's tools, but I had apparently neglected to say that almost none of them were in working order. George had a headache with all of them, but his nemesis was the chain saw. Whatever we had done to it was very obscure. He took it to pieces three times without discovering the difficulty.

George's theodolite fascinated me. He had the boys cut out a line of trees so that we could stand on our front steps and sight all the way across the plantation. His base line, as he called this, was a very important thing. It had to be accurate to a hair's breadth. He erected a large white marker to sight on at the other end of the plantation and spent four days orienting a key peg at our front steps. In this peg were some nails, painstakingly located to the last hair. I was embarrassed to tell him how happy I had been to come within three feet of a peg when I was surveying. Obviously our plantation was now in capable hands.

In order to keep Mabel and the children at a mutually respectful distance from each other, we decided to build the couple a house of their own.

I asked if they would like one of my father's design, similar to our own. To my surprise, I found that they preferred a Samoan fale, without sides. Their idea was to make a sort of Samoan-type resort hotel on the beautiful promontory above the waterfall. Tourists would love to sleep on innerspring mattresses in little fales lost among the trees. Mabel would run a central dining room where they could get the latest in tropical cooking. By the time they had finished describing it all, I was ready to book in myself. It certainly was the right type of project for Mabel.

A few days later the chain saw suddenly started working. To celebrate, George took a couple of the boys down to the promontory to clear a spot for their proposed resort.

"Why don't you go too, Mabel," I suggested. "You haven't set foot on the plantation yet. It's beautiful down there and you would be right with George."

A shout from Chippy, who was pounding on something by the front steps, made up her mind. She changed to her walking suit and leashed the dachshunds. They certainly could not be left to the tender mercies of the children.

"Maybe she will learn to like it here, after all," I thought as she turned down the drive.

Half an hour later I saw her tottering up the road. Her hair was disheveled and her face distraught. She had only one dog. I raced out to meet her. "What's the matter?" I cried.

All I could get out of her was a groaning sound between great gasps for air. I guided her into the house and lowered her onto the couch. She lay inert, rolling her eyes. Finally, she began to sob wildly. She had let the dachshunds off their leash for a romp and one of the fat little ninnies had bounced right over the edge of the gorge.

"How far down did he fall?" I asked.

"I don't know," she wailed. "I didn't dare look over. My darling little darling is gone, go-o-one. I'll never see his swe-et little face again."

"Look," I said, matter of factly, "he certainly got caught in the first bush on the way down. All we need is a boy with a rope. The boys climb down there every day, and all they get is a rest."

I sent for Ula's brother who had proved himself good at rescues. The problem caused some mirth among the boys. I was sure they could get the dog, but only hoped they would bring him back as they found him. The boys were prejudiced against dogs who ate birthday cakes. In a few minutes Ula's brother was back with the silly little animal tucked backwards under his arm. The dog had been caught in a bush three feet below the edge, and had been too scared to move. Mabel seized him frantically and sobbed endearments into his velvet ear.

A few moments later George came striding up the road. I expected him to rush in to comfort his wife. Instead, when he reached the front steps he suddenly let out a howl of rage. We rushed to the door to see what he was looking at.

He was pointing to the key survey pin of his base line. Chippy had pounded it, with all its hairbreadth nails, clean into the ground. The base line was ruined.

A few days later we returned from Apia to find George and Mabel gone. They didn't say where they were going. In fact they didn't even say good-by. I could only hope they had found a real plantation.

CHAPTER NINETEEN

On Malaga

Six months after George and Mabel left, we got help from another source.

"Wonderful news," shouted Vai, jumping off the bus and running towards the house. "Your mother is coming in August."

I could have wept for joy. My mother is an adventurous soul. She once set sail for the island of Manua during a mid-Pacific storm in a forty-foot open boat and lying on a case of dynamite. She had also weathered a Communist revolution in Hangchow, and helped integrate South Carolina. I was sure she was thus equipped to give me some helpful suggestions on a simple problem like plantation administration. It would be good to have someone to talk to again. And the children did need an American grandmother to confront them with the idea of wearing clothes.

But where would we put her? George and Mabel had proved conclusively that two bedrooms were insufficient for two adults, four children, and all their guests. The living room was already fully occupied with an ever-changing collection of housegirls, relatives, and visiting chiefs.

An addition to the house was an overdue solution to our expanding needs. My father's tropical house design had served us so well that we decided to build another just like it in the back yard.

There were so many functions to go in the new house: an office, a garage, a room for the housegirls, a carpentry shop, a schoolroom, a storehouse, and more bedrooms for ourselves and the relatives. Vai looked sceptically at my designs.

"If you spread all that around the ground," he said, "there will be no room left for bananas on this plantation. Let's build a two-story house and save on roofing iron."

Even doubled like that we had to hire the Public Works bulldozer to level off the top of the hill for the site. Earth-moving was a long operation because it rained every day. And it was prolonged several weeks when Buddy dumped a can of water down the exhaust pipe into the tractor engine.

But when work did get started, the house went up quickly and we dedicated it the night my mother arrived. I was proud of our homestead now. We put a white ceiling in the old house and varnished the louvers and floors. The new Samoan matting that we added gave to the whole an oddly pleasing Japanese effect accentuated by the lack of furniture. My mother fitted right in, settling down cross-legged on the floor with the boys. She loved to hear them sing and they treated her with utmost deference as matriarch of the family.

Her first project was an extensive bit of sewing for the children. When they were in a more respectable condition she proceeded with their education in our new schoolroom. As soon as her classes began, we had applications from all the families up and down the road. Clearly no educational project in Samoa was apt to fail for lack of participants. To my surprise, Vai told our neighbors to wait.

"Let's not work your mother so hard," he explained to me. "It is high time we all took a vacation. A former teacher of mine and her daughter are coming from Hawaii in a fortnight. Let's celebrate by taking them all on a real Samoan visiting party to Savai'i with a talking chief and everything. You'll feel better about Samoan custom after that."

I was delighted. If Salani found visiting parties so pleasant, why shouldn't I? My mother also wanted to see more of real Samoan life.

What Samoans may lack in commercial enterprise they more than make up in hospitality. Through the centuries the Samoan visiting party, the *malaga*, has been crowned in a glory of lavish ritual. Visiting is the chief recreation of every true Samoan. Modern roads and buses just facilitate the process. Villages, families, societies, and friends seem to be always on the move.

It suddenly occurred to me that my greatest error had been to stay at home where the burden of all this ritual fell on me. Why hadn't I thought of going visiting myself? The process must work two ways. Clearly it was proper to return Taligi's earlier visit to us. Taking our own talking chief insured us full ceremonial treatment. I had carefully backed away from all ceremonies after my experience with Vai's saofa'i. They seemed to involve such an enormous outlay of beef and crackers. But now we were the visitors, Vai explained to me privately, the tables would be turned. If our talking chief knew his business the exchange should run in our favor. Anyway, it was a wonderful way to entertain our guests.

Taligi is a chief's wife—a genuine faletua. The prospect of our official visit did not frighten her in the least. She was delighted when we warned her we were coming. Vai hunted up the most dignified of talking chiefs to lead our party. Mino was a large and impressive gentleman. He

brought all the necessary accouterments of his office, a·
large tapa cloth to wind around his waist, a staff to lean
upon while discoursing, and a great fly switch of sennit
fibers which doubled as a scepter. Vai provided him with
silver change to be used as a *lafo*, a modern ceremonial
contribution of money to our host's village.

Vai's teacher and her daughter were ideal visitors, eager
to see how Vai had developed since his high school days,
and delighted to participate in a genuine malaga. My
mother practiced up on the proper forms of greeting. We
all hung flowers over our ears and around our necks and
sang to Vai's ukulele as our little boat bounded across the
strip of ocean separating Upolu from the larger but less
developed island of Savai'i.

Savai'i is meant for Samoans: no restaurants, no hotels,
no shops—nothing for tourists. But for guests, hospitality
is everywhere. At Tuasivi the Samoan doctor in charge of
the hospital invited us to spend the night. Anxious to make
us feel at home his wife produced a full American meal
that even Betty Crocker would have approved. It must have
involved considerable research on her part.

In the morning the doctor put a car at our disposal and
we started along the coastal road around the island. I was
amazed at the size of Savai'i. Ecologists who fear that Samoa
will be overpopulated in fifty years should take another look
at Savai'i. Almost the only villages are those along the
coastal road and even here we traveled for miles without
seeing a fale. On the inland side seven hundred square
miles of untouched forest sloped gently back to the central
mountaintops.

Towards the end of the afternoon our car suddenly
turned inland along a mud track. After half an hour of
bouncing we emerged from the trees into an open field.
Around us lay the village of Paia where Taligi and her hus-

Vasiliu

band, Lopeti, served together as pastor, schoolteacher, nurse, and general factotum.

Taligi's home was a complex of three fales connected together. The middle fale had two stories. Like all pastors' homes, it was a center of village life. As we approached we saw that the chiefs were sitting in the first house, laughing, rolling sennit twine on their tattooed thighs, and waiting for us. The women of the village were assembled in the kitchen house, while the young men were busy at the open oven behind. They had been there all day.

We entered the first fale. After shaking hands around the circle of chiefs, we seated ourselves at vacant posts amid pleasant banter and a general slapping of thighs. The high chief of Paia launched into the traditional flowery speech of welcome.

Eventually our own talking chief, Mino, replied with equal eloquence, meanwhile, flicking his fly switch casually over his shoulder. His speech had barely lasted five minutes when a Paia chief held up his hand to call a halt.

"Don't tell me they think Mino is no good," I whispered anxiously to Vai.

"Oh, no," Vai replied, "the high chief of Paia could tell from the way he was treating their ceremonial titles that he knew all about them. There was no use going on. It was a great compliment to stop him."

Mino tossed our gift into the center of the floor, and the chiefs divided it, thanking us profusely.

"Don't think we are paying for our visit," Vai whispered to me. "It's not that at all. Ceremonial money is just a form of politeness. You'll see."

After the welcome, their graceful Village Maiden, dressed in a towering headdress and fine mat, squeezed the kava. Then, as it was evening, the village served us with a special feast called a *sua*. There are many degrees of suas, I learned. The contents of ours and the way it was presented showed we ranked high in village esteem. A young woman laid a fine mat at Vai's feet. Another knelt with a pierced coconut. Then we were presented with a leaf tray of taro and chicken. Finally the young men carried in a whole roast pig on a litter. It had been cooking all day on the hot rocks of the oven.

The conversation that evening centered about a cave in the mountains above Paia. The "little people" had been seen there again. When I asked about these "little people" I learned that the cave was inhabited by little men about three feet high who were full of mischief. My mother and I immediately expressed a desire to make their acquaintance, and a chief volunteered to take us to the cave the next day.

Equipped with flashlights and lanterns we started up the mountain in the morning. The teacher and I chatted knowledgeably about the myths and fantasies of simple peoples as we mounted the trail.

I had never seen a cave like this one. We climbed down a small grassy hole, and suddenly found ourselves in a long tube about twelve feet in diameter and perfectly rounded. Its smooth walls stretched both ways into the blackness. For about a mile we walked easily down this natural corridor. Suddenly the tube came to a sharp edge as if the end of the tube had been broken off by a giant hand. We let ourselves down cautiously over the edge into the darkness and splashed into a pool of water twelve feet below.

The edge of the pool was thick with mud as we climbed out. I turned my flashlight down to help extricate my feet and what I saw stopped me dead! There before me in the mud was a tiny footprint about 2½ inches long, with a heel and five perfect toes. I swallowed twice and looked again. There was another and another, a right and a left. They were running everywhere. Speechless, I looked at our guide, and pointed a trembling forefinger at the prints.

"Don't be frightened," he nodded knowingly. "The little people are frisky but they never hurt anybody."

The teacher and I examined the footprints carefully. If there were a natural explanation for these perfect little prints we could not think of it, but we spoke no more of simple people and their fantasies.

When we returned to Paia in the afternoon we discovered that several families had brought gifts in our absence. Four or five large pigs, a barrel of beef, baskets of taro, and leaf packages of fish lay on the grass before the fale. We feasted again and Mino distributed what was left over to the village.

So it went for four days. One evening we had a special supper of *pisua*, a gooey, chewy mass of arrowroot and coconut cream, served in washbasins and eaten with the fingers. Another afternoon a line of women crossed the green carrying food and mats in a presentation called *si'ilaulau*. At another time the men of the village gave us a *laulau tasi*. A talking chief opened each of their baskets as they arrived and announced the contents to the village in a loud voice. Those who brought the most probably gained great prestige. But I began to feel guilty and a little uncomfortable. Undeniably we were an economic drain on the whole village. The exchange had certainly turned in our favor. But I heard no complaints. Everyone seemed anxious to have us stay.

Gayest of all was the final feast and entertainment on the eve of our departure. At sunset the girls of the village came with a mountain of gifts: forty bottles of fragrant oil, a dozen feathered fans, softly woven pandanus baskets, sleeping mats, tapas, and shell necklaces. Then the boys arrived with food: roast pigs, crabs, lobsters, chop suey, salt beef, and cakes. My mother and I especially enjoyed a crisp little hors d'oeuvrelike delicacy until we discovered that it was fried worm.

After the feast the young men, decked in flowers, appeared with guitars, ukuleles, and a kerosene drum. Dancing and singing began, first the girls' side, then the boys'. The children of the village crowded in around the edges, laughing and clapping. Babies in their mothers' arms crowed with delight. Everyone participated right up to the grandmothers, who specialized in comic dancing. Never have I seen a party so spontaneous, so effortless, so full of life of every age and description. At midnight the village maiden appeared, glistening with fragrant oil and shining *ti* leaves. Flat brown nuts clacked on her ankles and mirrors twinkled from her headdress. The young men broke into a chant and even the babies opened their great brown eyes with admiration as she opened the final siva dance with a barely perceptible flick of the wrist.

I felt happy but humble. With all my education and capital had I provided Taligi and her retinue even a fraction of this generosity and pleasure at my home? I, with all my superior resources, felt poor and insecure. She, with nothing but the respect of her village, obviously felt rich. Maybe the difference was that she was part of a tribe. I was merely one lonely individual.

Early in the morning the village boys shouldered pigs, roast chickens, cases of biscuits, kegs of beef, and baskets of gifts on their carrying poles, and led us a mile or so down through the forests to catch the bus.

"We have enough food here to feed Lafulemu for a month," I remarked to Vai. "It more than makes up for your saofa'i."

"Don't count your pigs till they get home," he suggested with a knowing smile.

Wherever we paused along the homeward route, relatives ran out to shake our hands. We handed them baskets of food and little gifts. When Mino, our talking chief, left us at Salelalogo, he commandeered the fine mats, the pigs, the kegs of beef, the biscuits, and the gifts. I tucked a small bottle of oil into my bag as the booty was unloaded. It was just as well to have one souvenir. That bottle and one small leg of one small pig was all that ever reached Lafulemu.

The last night of our malaga we spent with Vai's parents on the island of Manono, which is between the two large islands. Manono is a one-square-mile gem of untouched tropical beauty, mounted in dazzlingly white sand and dropped into an ocean of brilliant blue.

In the evening Vai and I walked along the beach together. In a Maxfield Parrish sky Venus hung close enough to touch. The trade wind wafted the evening hymns to us from the little fales around the village square. Fishermen's torches glided like stars over the water. It was fairyland.

I took the hand of my matai and suddenly my heart relaxed to the Samoan way. I stopped worrying about whether it would work. My tensions with it slipped away. In my harried effort to make it more prosperous and productive, I had apparently overlooked the fact that Samoa had a perfection and completeness all of its own.

What was it Vai had said about wanting independence so that Samoa could set its own goals and give its own answers? If pleasure of close companionship was the goal, Samoa had found the answer. It was living according to its own genius. Unwittingly I had presumed that progress and prosperity were the goals of everyone. They weren't.

No longer did I try to comfort myself with the fragile hope that "we are all alike under the skin." My experiences seemed to reveal how surprisingly different Samoans and Americans were in their ideas of property, propriety, child raising, and the purpose of life.

But what was so bad about that? True, I had had my surprises and frustrations when we tried living together. The problems of supplying Samoan feasts, raising Samoan children, predicting Samoan behavior, and running commercial

enterprises were all too real. But in return I had been exposed to an exciting discovery. The range, and depth, and
possibilities of the human soul were so much more vast and
promising than I had ever conceived. While my American
culture was pioneering the way towards human prosperity
through the release of the individual, Samoan culture was
making its own valid discoveries about the human satisfaction and security of close communal relationships. How
much we would lose if we were both the same! Wasn't I
a warmer, wiser, happier person for having lived with my
matai?

LaVergne, TN USA
19 October 2010
201446LV00001B/80/P